THE THREE LIVES OF MY FATHER

FROM FEIVEL PITUM TO PHILIP HALPERN

By

Barry S. Halpern

THE THREE LIVES OF MY FATHER. by Barry S. Halpern

Library of Congress Control Number: 2011910695

First edition
ISBN 978-1463561710

Cover photograph from Philip Halpern's naturalization certificate (1942)

e-mail: **feivel.pitum@gmail.com**
website: **feivelpitum.bbnow.org**

To my father Feivel Pitum, who continues to inspire me;

To my children and my (yet unborn) grandchildren, who keep Feivel alive within them;

To continuing his quest: never forget where we come from, who we are and what we owe to those who came before.

TABLE OF CONTENTS

Appendices

1. The Pitum Family History – A Conjectural History
   Generation by Generation
2. Timeline/Key Events in life of Philip Halpern
3. Sample writings of Philip Halpern

   Adult Jewish Education – April, 1963

   There is no "Negro Problem

   As I See It – 1964

   It's Amazing

   Passover Thoughts

   JFK Tribute – 1963

   "The Bible and the Twist"

   A Controversial Play – 1964

   A Jew Looks Toward the Ecumenical Council - 1963

   Editorial Regarding Black Muslims – 1964

   Miscellaneous notes and Correspondence
4. Isadore Zack – a brief biography
5. Anti Defamation League speakers – a selection

   Ephraim Isaac – Ethiopian Jewry – 1964

   David Chajmowixz – Cuban Jewry – 1964

   Pho Ba Hai – Vietnamese – 1965

   Haskell Kassler – civil rights attorney – 1958
6. Pedigree chart for Feivel Pitum - conjectural
7. Miscellaneous documents and maps
8. Sources and Bibliography

PREFACE

"Intelligence is a source of life unto its possessor. The heart of the wise maketh its mouth intelligent. And upon his lips, he increaseth information." (1963 profile of Philip Halpern; quote taken from the Book of Proverbs)

My father slid the short stack of four quarters across the bridge table. He gave me a look that at the time made me wonder what he was thinking. I know that he was sorry it was only the four quarters and not the eight that was my normal weekly allowance. As I looked into his eyes, though, they showed more than regret. They showed sadness. Sadness about what I didn't know, nor am I even certain I recognized their sadness at the time.

It was about 2:30 on a quiet Sunday afternoon, January 23, 1966. There was a moderate snowstorm starting up outside our apartment on the second floor of a two family home at 200 Blue Hills Parkway in Milton, Massachusetts. We were in our small den, with a bridge table set up to use as a counting surface for the weekly take from the two self service laundromats that my father owned, one in Nantasket (the "Surfside Laundromat"), and the other in Framingham (both in the Boston, Massachusetts metropolitan area). Our black and white television was on, but I don't remember the program.

My father would make the round trip of more than 80 miles from Milton to Nantasket to Framingham at least once a day. Often he would have to make the circuit twice in one day. Every Sunday when the stores were closed, he'd empty the coins from all of the machines and do the weekly count. During the summer beach season in Nantasket, the stores would remain open and the emptying would have to happen early morning or late at night. Frequently I would go with him to help and thus would increase my chances of adding some unusual coins to my small coin collection. I knew that as a family we didn't have much money but that the summer months always produced the largest take, and the mid-winter months very little. That was why it made sense for my allowance to sometimes be reduced.

I was thirteen years old at the time and had just become a Bar Mitzvah two months prior to that Sunday. Looking back at the photos now it's easy to see how proud both of my parents were at the time. My father's smile was beaming.

November 20, 1965 - My Bar Mitzvah

I was an only child and I think I knew at the time that I was spoiled. Not with money, but with love. I could do just about anything I wanted, and ask for and get just about anything. I'm sure I didn't feel that way at the time, but looking back, well...

I knew that my father was in debt, though I didn't know by how much. I knew that he worked hard every day. I knew that both of my parents participated in volunteer Jewish organizations. My mother was a member of ORT – the Organization for Rehabilitation and Training - and of B'nai B'rith. My father was a member of the Anti-Defamation League and Jeremiah Lodge (a men's version of B'nai B'rith). At the time, though, I had no idea what they actually did for

—

these organizations. It did seem to me that they spent a lot of time on them, and that their activities were important both to them and to the others with whom they worked.

My mother came from a very large family; she was one of thirteen children. She was born in Boston but lived her early years in Concord, New Hampshire until moving back to Boston. I had aunts, uncles, and many cousins all over the Boston area and it seemed that every week we'd be with at least a dozen or more of them. At times during my childhood some of us even lived in the same house in Dorchester at 80 Esmond Street. My count of first cousins, which included some related by marriage, was in the 40s! There were also a few "first cousins, once removed", many of whom were more of my generation than some of my first cousins. So despite being an only child, I rarely felt alone.

I knew that my father had very few relatives, with my proof of that being the very few visits we'd have with one or two of his uncles. But there were no first cousins from his side of the family. My father was born in another country, though I don't believe that at that time I even knew the name of that country (Lithuania). It never occurred to me that my father Philip Halpern had been born with a different name. I also knew that he had served in the US Army. Uncle Julius (Baron) was the relative from my father's side of the family who I saw most often; he was actually my Great Uncle. We would visit his home frequently on Sunday afternoons and I was in awe of his den and library. It seemed as though he had hundreds or thousands of books there and I remember always thinking that someday I wanted to have a library like that one. He had a very deep, throaty voice and I have never forgotten the way he sounded.

Back to that Sunday so long ago…

About 6:30 in the evening, my father went outside to brush the snow off the car – it had been snowing steadily throughout the afternoon. On the television was the old show "Science Fiction Theater". A few minutes later my father came

3

inside, holding his left arm and seemingly unable to walk up the stairs. I later learned that earlier in the week, at least two times, his arm had been feeling numb and he and my mother had talked about the need for him to take some time from work and see the doctor (our family doctor had the unusual name of "Doctor Saver" – I wish he had been there that night). My father was always working so hard during the day that I believe he put off visits to doctors and dentists as often as he could.

From that moment on the stairway, it all happened so quickly. The ambulance, the Milton Hospital emergency room, the doctors going in, coming out, and by 8:30 he was gone. The final time I saw him lasted maybe 60 seconds – they thought he was improving so they let me in to see him. He took my hand, I kissed him, he told me that he loved me and I said the same thing back to him. I was ushered out and then I heard the vomiting and the retching; one of the nurses in the emergency room said to me that this was a "good sign", but it certainly didn't sound like a good sign to me. It only lasted a few minutes, and then it was over. He was 50 years old and had no previous (diagnosed) history of heart disease. In fact, I don't remember ever seeing him sick.

So that Sunday evening started me (and my mother) on a new road in our lives. We held onto the laundries for a couple of years. I worked almost every day after school, driving to either Framingham or Nantasket. Then we sold them, first the business in Framingham and then the one in Nantasket. My mother got a "real" job, a good job with the State of Massachusetts that would ultimately provide her with fantastic lifetime health insurance benefits and a very small pension. My father's $20,000 of life insurance paid off his debts though there was nothing left over. What remained were his enduring love and the examples that he set for me, many of which would not become apparent to me until later in my life.

That Sunday in 1966 is now more than 45 years in the past. For most of those 45 years I knew very little about my father's past life. He never spoke about it to me, and my mother either didn't know that much or didn't talk about it. Or I simply never asked. However, for the past few years, through

—

a series of fortuitous genealogical research efforts, I've been able to piece together some of my father's story.

What follows is that story. It's incomplete and probably raises more questions than it answers. However, it sheds light on areas that were dark for most of my life. Through my research and discoveries, I have learned more about myself because now I know more about where my father came from, who he was and even what he thought. Through my journey of discovery of my father and his past, I've learned about not just the people, places and things that shaped his life, but I've gained some insights into his thoughts and dreams...

INTRODUCTION - MY SEARCH FOR FEIVEL PITUM

The study of genealogy takes on aspects of both art and science. When beginning a project, the researcher must follow a step-by-step, scientific approach in digging through the past. The "art" of the search comes into play as the researcher becomes more of a detective than a pure researcher. Take a scrap of evidence here, find an old, torn photo there, and piece together the story as best as possible.

The genealogist will almost always create a "family tree" or "pedigree chart" that lists his or her ancestors as far back in time as the research allows. Through this art and science of genealogy the researcher hopes to piece together a "family history". It might be a narrative about the particular family in question, and it may provide pure scientific data and facts about that family, as well as stories and tales and suppositions that have been passed on from generation to generation. Some family histories can contain volumes about literally thousands of ancestors, depending upon the available records and information that has been passed down. Or they can be relatively brief stories about only a few individuals.

This book presents my own family history, a story about my father, Feivel Pitum, later called Philip Halpern.

I had joined the internet site "www.jewishgen.org" (or "Jewishgen") probably in 1997 or 1998, but for years had not found any useful information regarding the Pitum family name or possible paternal ancestors of mine. During my father's lifetime, he spoke very little (to me) of his life in Lithuania, at least nothing that I can recall. Even his life prior to marrying my mother was a mystery to me. When he died in 1966, I was not very curious about discovering his past, though I would sometimes fleetingly wonder about it. Like many people, I just never pursued it because I was simply too busy with other things in my life to which I attached higher priorities (my studies, my job, my family, etc.) Even though I spent more than eighteen years living and working outside of the United States, in Asia, I never thought much about Eastern Europe, its history, or how it related to my father and his family.

—

When my mother passed away in 2007 and I began to go through her things, I found some items that had belonged to my father. Some of these things I had seen before, but I hadn't paid much attention to them. There was a wallet from the ship *Britannic* (the ship that brought my father from Europe to the United States in 1934), and I knew that it had some documents in it, but they were in Hebrew or Yiddish and the handwriting was virtually illegible, so I ignored them.

So at that time, what I knew about my father was that he was born in Lithuania, in a small town called Aukstadvaris (also referred to in Yiddish or Russian as Visokidvor). I knew that he had come to the United States as a young adult, joined the army, and that his family had been murdered and buried in mass graves. I also knew that he had a younger sister who had survived and was living in the USSR, and was hoping to move to Israel at some point. I also had seen and heard him referring to his "original" name as Feivel Pitum but I hadn't thought anything of that. The conversations regarding his name centered on his Hebrew name, Shraga (or Shrago) Feivel Ben (son of) Dov Ber, which I had seen written in both Hebrew and English. These few facts are the only ones I knew of my father's history.

On and off through the years, I would log into Jewishgen, do a Pitum family search, and come up empty. In 1999, my mother's family, the Waldmans, had a reunion attended by more than 250 of my relatives. During that event, I learned of my mother's family's history (her family also came from Lithuania) and their shtetl (Jewish village) of Valkininkai (Olkeniki). The Waldman family had been traced to the late 1700's, which seemed impressive to me, and I began to wonder more about my father's history. This was also my first exposure or realization that Eastern European town names were not unique – that is, the names could be in Lithuanian, Polish, Russian, Yiddish, Hebrew and other languages, making it much more difficult for some to locate their ancestral origins. I was fortunate in that I knew the names of the shtetls for both my mother and my father.

Over time, I had purchased a few books about Lithuania and Lithuanian Jewry but never thought I'd be able to find out any more. After all, weren't all the records destroyed during the Holocaust? Weren't the families all murdered, their possessions plundered? At least that was the "common wisdom", and remains one of the common myths today.

It was on Yom Kippur day in 2009 when I was at home in Boulder, Colorado instead of in a synagogue where I was supposed to be, that my past, or rather my father's past, surprisingly opened up to me. A search on Jewishgen turned up the Pitum name for the first time, with some family tree information that mentioned my father's uncle Julius Baron, and also had some other Pitums in it. The dates seemed right, the town – Aukstadvaris – was right. It appeared to me that someone had traced their family tree and it linked to my family.

I sent off a quick email to the researcher listed on the web site, Eden Joachim. One of the nice features of Jewishgen (and various other genealogical research web sites) is that they make a provision for you to contact "researchers" who are looking into either your family name or shtetl or country. The initial contact is anonymous, until there is a response. I've subsequently used this method to make contact with several other people who I have helped or who have helped me.

In my email, I wrote about who I was and how I thought I might be related to the same Pitums in her research. She wrote back a few hours later and confirmed that I apparently had two living first cousins who were the children of my father's sister Leah. I had such a mixture of emotions for this Yom Kippur! I knew I had all those cousins from the Waldman side of my family, but never imagined I had cousins from my father's side! I continued my internet search – all of this happening on that same Yom Kippur day – and found an email address for Zalman Lazkovich. I wrote to him, introduced myself and said that I thought we might be first cousins.

The rest is history, or rather, genealogy. That's what led me to discover the linkage to my father's family. It turns out that Eden is my third cousin. Through the information that Zalman had provided to Eden for Jewishgen, I was able to get

—

the names of my father's family. These names required no research or validation - he was our personal source and he had known those names his entire life. He knew the names of his mother's parents and grandparents. There were also a couple of dates provided which proved helpful in my subsequent research. Of course, for a proper genealogical study, it's more prudent to obtain birth, death and marriage certificates. But at this point, I was thrilled to have finally learned at least the names of my previously "secret" paternal grandparents.

As for tracing my father's family back even further, more work and time was required. From that Yom Kippur day onwards, I bought more books on genealogy and on Lithuania, discovered more internet sites (ancestry.com, footnote.com, ellisisland.org, stevemorse.org, etc.), and learned about various SIGs ("special interest groups") that are dedicated to one or more areas of Jewish genealogical research. I joined two local Jewish genealogy clubs, one in Boston and one in Colorado. Also very important, I bought a large whiteboard and a package of markers. They would be used in writing down every bit of information I would be learning, and then connecting lines and people to paint a picture of what would turn out to be my father's family tree. I began to organize my rapidly growing collection of paper into files. I began to organize my expanding electronic files into genealogy folders on my computer. I purchased my first Apple computer, a Macbook, because I wanted to use the genealogy software package called "Reunion", which also enabled me to access the very large database (much of which was put together by the genealogist and family friend David Kanter, who helped to inspire me to push forward with my own research) containing my mother's genealogical research.

All of these resources led me to obtain some of the "vital records" from Lithuania – including the 1858 "Revision List" (a sort of census), as well as another one going back to 1811. These Excel spreadsheets contain translations of the original records from various Lithuanian towns (which may have been written in Russian, Hebrew or Yiddish), and identify family names, members of households, ages, relationships to the heads of households, and even some marriage record

—

information. I obtained them by becoming a member (via a modest monetary contribution) of the online Litvak Special Interest Group (LitvakSIG), though as time goes on many of these records become available to the general public simply by registering at Jewishgen.

A common phrase amongst genealogical researchers is "brick wall". That is, every researcher ultimately progresses to a certain point and cannot get past it. We try to go around it, over it, under it, back away and then try to slam right through it. It could be that we are able to trace our family back to an ancestor's arrival in the United States, but we don't know his or her original name and thus we get stuck. It may be that we know the original name and town from Europe, but don't have any further information because it was a small town with little to no surviving information. Unfortunately, what happens in these cases is that we frequently get tired, stressed, frustrated, and want to give up. We usually move on to something else and then come back later (hours, days or months), and hope that something will be different. In my case, I eventually was able to break through the wall brick by brick.

With my search for the Pitum family, a marriage record (located via LitvakSIG) for Feivel's parents enabled me to figure out that his father didn't come from Aukstadvaris, but from Stakliskes (Stoklishok), a nearby shtetl. I had previously been looking for the wrong town!

Moving backwards in time from here is problematic. At one point, I firmly believed that I had traced my father's paternal ancestry back several more generations, to an Abram Pitum, probably born around the year 1760. In fact, I still believe that my father and I are descended from an Abram Pitum. However, as I write this, I cannot be certain and cannot "prove" it. Thus, I am at yet another brick wall. We believe we have enough information to be able to draw various conclusions, but we are missing key pieces, or we are faced with conflicting information. We suspect we're correct, but enough doubt remains that further investigation is needed.

Therefore, within the main text of this book, I describe my father's genealogy only back to his great-grandparents, about whom I am certain of the details. In the Appendix, I present what I am calling my "conjectural genealogy", which still requires further proof. In any event, even if this "conjectural" tracing is not correct in the names and people I've listed, it is likely that Feivel's actual ancestors were similar to those described. They lived in the same towns, they had similar names, their day-to-day lives were similar and they were neighbors of the people I've described.

My internet research, combined with closer readings of Philip's papers that my mother had saved, enabled me to learn more about the ship "*Britannic*", which was my father's transport across the Atlantic. I was able to locate the ship manifest from Feivel's first arrival in the United States at the port of Boston. Thanks to my membership in the Jewish Genealogy Society of Colorado, I met someone (Shai Kowitt) who was able to translate some of my father's writings from the ship. It was a draft of more than one letter (my father wrote and saved many drafts of his writings). The translation enabled me to find out more about his involvement in a Zionist youth movement (the Gordonia). I was able to digitize and enhance a 1966 audio recording that I had made, which enabled me to discover my father's relationship with his friend Isadore Zack, his role in military intelligence, and his passion for Judaism and Zionism. Newsletters from the men's group my father belonged to, the Jeremiah Lodge, enabled me to learn more about his thinking and his remarkable writing ability.

From his translated letter, he references an activity in the summer of 1933 which sounds like a Zionist youth camp. A group photograph of a Gordonia summer youth camp, found on the US Holocaust Museum web site, contains a young man who strongly resembles my father. However, I can't be 100% certain that he is the person I see in the photograph. If not, the activities illustrated are certainly consistent with his wishes and desires. He could have attended that camp, or one like it. He certainly participated in a very influential program in 1933; if not the one in the photograph, then another one.

Each time one of my "bricks" fell, it was an emotional moment for me. My first reading of the translated letter he had

---

11

written on his ship to the United States opened up some incredible insights. It was as though he were telling me his story. I could hear his voice, complete with his Lithuanian Jewish accent. Listening to my tape of Isadore Zack memorialize my father in 1966 opened a flood of memories and revelations. Reading samples of his writings again made me feel as though I was actually listening to him talking to me.

There still remain so many gaps, unknowns, and uncertainties in his life story. I have yet to trace his maternal line. I know so little about his pre-marriage years in the United States. I know so little about his childhood in Aukstadvaris. Perhaps I will never know. Despite these shortcomings, what I've found has enabled me to at least document in this book some of my father's life so that his descendants can better know their grandfather.

After I began preparing this book, I discovered a trove of additional writings and related materials of my father, contained within some of the boxes that my mother had saved. I was struck by the fact that he had saved his drafts, in some cases at least three of them. Some were handwritten and some were typed. I found early versions of some of the editorials that were ultimately printed in the Jeremiah Lodge newsletters. I also found additional materials on a range of topics; for some of these, I don't know whether or not they were ultimately published or whether my father was just writing for the "fun" of it.

In particular, I discovered several writings and correspondence related to guest speakers at his Lodge's breakfast meetings. These were people he introduced at the Lodge's breakfast meetings. I don't actually know whether he recruited them or not, but he clearly got to know them at least a little bit before he put himself out in public to introduce them. The range of speakers was interesting in and of itself. There was a civil rights lawyer who had been beaten in Mississippi while representing clients (the lawyer was from Boston). There was a Vietnamese graduate student, who later went on to become a leader of the Vietnamese community in New England. There was a Jewish Community leader from Cuba who lived there both before and during the Castro regime.

While most of Phil's writings and activities were related to Judaism and Jews in some fashion, they clearly broadened to civil rights, basic human freedoms, race relations, and a desire for a more humanitarian and progressive world. For me, reading through the materials has been eye-opening, as I see in myself quite a bit of what my father wrote and believed. I can't imagine that I learned much of my own views from him directly. I certainly wasn't reading what he wrote at the time, nor did I read it in any depth until very recently. But somehow he passed all of this along to me, and I absorbed it.

A "living" source: Isadore Zack

As I mentioned earlier, the keynote speaker at the Jeremiah Lodge memorial service for my father in 1966 was Isadore Zack. I remembered that he and my dad were good friends, but I didn't know anything about him or how he met my father. I had recorded the memorial breakfast meeting using my then relatively new Concord brand reel-to-reel tape recorder, which has been remarkably preserved and continues to operate almost as well as in 1966. Listening to that recording, and Iz's story about himself and my dad, I realized that they were army buddies who had first met in 1941 - and therefore remained friends for the 25 years remaining in my father's life.

My father befriended Iz Zack in 1941 long before he met my mother or any of my other relatives. I realized that if I could find him, I would be speaking with someone who is a living link to my father's past. A living link that takes me back further than any other person alive today! There are very few other people still alive who even knew my father, and virtually all of them did not meet him until 1950 or later. Isadore Zack pre-dates them by almost ten years.

How was I able to find my father's friend? My search on the internet helped me to learn of his role in military intelligence. My father's papers and notes had frequent references to Iz as well as correspondence with him. I was able to determine that Iz was 98 years old (in 2010), and still alive

13

and thriving in Quincy, Massachusetts, only minutes from Milton where I had grown up and where I still visit my in-laws several times a year. I phoned him and we spoke for a few minutes. He was thrilled to hear from me and urged that I come visit as quickly as possible. Though he protested that physically he wasn't so well, mentally he was 100%. So I made a special trip to Boston and visited for about 90 minutes with Iz and his wife Ruth. He greeted me at the door (physically he appeared healthy and almost robust) and quickly sat me down and began talking. When I say that he "quickly sat me down", I mean that within two minutes of my ringing the doorbell we were already sitting in his living room, my digital recorder was turned on, and in a loud and strong voice and Boston accent, he began...

"Yawh fah-thah was drafted in Mahtch nineteen fawty-one! Practically the same day I was drafted. Maybe a day aftah. He wound up at the 26th infantry division at Camp Edwahds."

His memories of my father were crisp and clear and he told stories of the two of them and others. It was a fascinating day that in many ways added to my knowledge about my father, and also confirmed my appreciation of him.

One of Iz's stories was about a photograph of Phil that Iz couldn't locate prior to my visiting him. He said that the photo had been taken just after my father's arrival overseas in the European theater, and it showed him standing in front of the Alps. Phil had sent Iz the photo in 1944 (Iz remained Stateside during the war, fulfilling his role in military intelligence). After my visit with Iz, I returned home to Colorado and pulled out the very few photos I had of my father in the army, and there was the photo! Just as Isadore Zack had described, my father was standing there in a field, mountains behind him, the war in front of him.

Later in this book, I'll write more about what I learned from Iz Zack that day, as well as how he and my father interacted during their lifetime.

The Three Lives of Feivel Pitum

This book is about my journey into a past that I thought no longer existed. My father's and his family's past. My search has found that I was wrong – his past does exist and this book attempts to present some parts of it. My search has also been a journey of discovery for me as I learned more and more about where he and his parents and their parents came from, the towns they lived in, how they lived and how they died. Regrettably, I do not have any "personal" details about the lives of my ancestors, nor have I located any photographs. But I know some of their names, and I know when and where they lived. I can make inferences about how they lived, and as a result of my research I have learned so much more about my "roots" than I ever thought possible.

I started this project intending to write a genealogical story of the Pitum family. Instead, this has turned into more of a story about my father than about his ancestors, though the family genealogical history I've discovered laid a foundation which enabled me to tell a much better tale about my father.

My father's and his family's birthplace is the country of Lithuania. As I mentioned, I was very surprised to discover that his father had been born not in Aukstadvaris but in Stakliskes. Finding this information enabled me to trace the names and birth years of his ancestors through to my paternal great-grandfather.

I am very confident, though admittedly not 100% so, that the family lineage I present in the conjectural genealogy in the Appendix is accurate. It is based on some personal details that I have known about, as well as details provided by my first cousin, Zalman Lazkovich. Zalman is the son of my father's sister Leah, who survived the holocaust and killings in Lithuania and eventually immigrated to Israel. Through them, I know the names of my grandparents and great-grandparents.

Through DNA testing it may be possible to locate a previously unknown relative who may have more information about their ancestry. Thus far, I haven't been able to make any momentous discoveries. I've been fortunate to have a couple of fairly strong matches of my DNA with a few other people. However, our names and ancestry provide no clues as to how we are actually related. It is likely to pre-date the mid-1700s. There is some evidence that our families originated in Spain and therefore possibly we were Sephardic Jews rather than Ashkenazim, but this is mainly speculation.

My father's story is best told in three stages, as his life was pretty much divided into three parts, of roughly equal length. There was his childhood "first life" in Lithuania as Feivel Pitum, lasting from 1915 to 1934. There was his "second life" beginning with his arrival in the United States in 1934 and the changing of his name to Philip Halpern. This period lasted through his service in the military and ended with his marriage to my mother in 1950. Finally, his "third life" began in 1950 and continued until his death in 1966.

Throughout my story, the only person I mention who knew my father for more than one of his "lives" was Isadore Zack, who met him in 1941 during Philip's second life, and knew and worked with him during his third life, until his death in 1966.

In presenting my father's story, I struggled a bit with how to write the names of people and towns. The history of the Jewish people in Lithuania, and of Lithuania itself, involves the use of a variety of languages and spellings to describe the same person or place. For example, my father was born in the town of Aukstadvaris. Or rather the town of Visokidvor, or Wisokidwor. Or various other spellings. His birth surname was "Pitum", or "Pitumaite", or "Pitem". His first identifiable male ancestor according to my "conjectural" history was "Abram" (or "Avram" or "Abraham"). His great grandfather was known as "Arie" or "Leyba" or "Arie Leib" or perhaps other names, but all of them refer to the same individual. Languages in use were Lithuanian, Yiddish, Russian, German, Hebrew, and perhaps others. In any event, I've tried to use what seems appropriate in context, even if not entirely consistent.

As to my father's original given name, a few observations are needed. I have seen the English version of his original name spelled as Faivel, Faivl, Favriel, Faviel, Faivel, Feivelius, and probably others. For this book, I have chosen the spelling "Feivel", because that is the way he wrote it in the US, it's the way my mother wrote it, and it is a common US spelling of the original Yiddish name.[1] The name itself originates from the Aramaic, meaning "candle" or "light", which I think is very appropriate for my father as he was indeed a "light" for all of those with whom he came into contact.

Any search for a family history requires a lot of detective work. You start with very little and know almost nothing. You take a piece of this, a scrap of that, put them together and you create a picture that speaks far more than 1,000 words. It's enjoyable. It's tedious. It's tiring and frustrating. It's addictive. In the end, it's fantastically rewarding and fulfilling.

If there are errors in my writings or my research, those errors are all mine. Readers should feel free to let me know of any corrections or additional information. In future editions (if there are any) I will do what I can to correct and update what is contained here.

---

[1] Jewishgen.org, the Lithuanian Given Names Database

Top: Isadore Zack when I met with him in 2010

Bottom: Phil Halpern in 1944 with the Alps as backdrop

THE PITUM FAMILY HISTORY

Generation by Generation

To set the stage for this story, it's necessary to first look at the Pitum family tree in order to better place my father within the context of his family. I have been able to positively identify five generations of Pitums in my father's family history. I am the fourth generation and my children are the fifth. Unfortunately, there is precious little information available about my father's parents, and their parents and grandparents. However, my search was able to discover some of their names, their birthplaces, as well as a few other details. There are no photos and no stories. Some general information is available about the towns they lived in, including some Jewish history. As Lithuania was under several different governments during the past 250 or so years, the town names and even the people's names sometimes present themselves in a very confusing manner. The cities of Trakai and Vilnius, which are the closest "large" cities to Stakliskes and Stoklishok, have been called Troki and Vilna. I've mentioned previously that even the surname Pitum can be seen with differing spellings - Pitem, Pittum - and pronunciations: Pitumaite. In Hebrew, the word "pitum" means the tip of a fruit, and the name was most commonly found in the region around Troki/Trakai, Lithuania[2].

What follows is what I've learned thus far. While the facts are sparse, they are nonetheless facts. These are my ancestors. A family tree or "pedigree chart" is provided in the appendix as an aide.

---

[2] Beider, Alexander. *A Dictionary of Jewish Surnames from the Russian Empire.* Avotaynu, 1993.

The Pitum family as I know it originated in the small Lithuanian town of Stakliskes (Yiddish), also known as Stoklishok (Lithuanian). Lithuania's history is one of changing borders and governments, at one time independent, then under Poland or Russia, and then independent again. Names and spellings of towns depend upon sources, which could be Yiddish, Lithuanian, or Russian. In this book, I am using names that I am most familiar with, although referencing alternate names when appropriate. Hopefully what I've used will be clear to the reader.

Stakliskes is located within the Troki (Trakai) and Vilnius (Vilna) district (or "guberniya") depending upon the timeframe. The town had a Jewish population that approached 1,000 by the year 1900, and at various times comprised 30-40% of the total population. By World War II there were only about 70 Jewish families remaining. [3]

The use of surnames was not common amongst Jews in

---

[3] Spector, Shmuel, and Geoffrey Wigoder. *The Encyclopedia of Jewish Life Before and During the Holocaust*. New York University Press, 2001.

Eastern Europe until well into the 1800s. In Lithuania, they were not even required until the early 1800s, and implementation varied by location within the country. Jews were normally known by their lineage. For example, my name in Hebrew is "Dov Ber ben Shraga Feivel." The Hebrew "Ben" means "son of". My father's Hebrew name was "Shraga Feivel ben Dov Ber." Note the "reversal" of names by generation. Also important is that Jews were not named after living relatives. So it is highly unlikely for a Jewish person to hold the name of his or her mother or father, though it did occur in instances where the father died during the wife's pregnancy, or the mother died during childbirth.

First generation (Arie Leib PITUM)

Arie Leib Pitum, my great-grandfather, was probably born during the 1850s, in Stakliskes, though we do not have his exact birth year. It was common for Jews to have "double names" (e.g. Arie Leib, Dov Ber). The first is the Hebrew name; the second is the Yiddish name. In English, the name "Arie" (and Leib) means "lion". In my own case, "Dov Ber", both names mean "bear" in English, and I am named after my grandfather. I am proud to know that I am descended from a lion and a bear.

Second generation (Berka PITUM)

Arie Lieb married a woman named Feiga. Their marriage produced at least one son: Berka Pitum, my grandfather, born in 1891. Berka Pitum also was known by the names Berka, Beryl and Dov Ber. Lithuanian records indicate that this birth was in Stakliskes.

Third generation (Feivel PITUM)

Berka Pitum married Asnat Baron. She was born in 1890, and is listed (in Lithuanian records) as being born in the town of Traby, although her parents and other relatives all seem to have been born in Aukstadvaris. Perhaps she was born during a brief visit away from Aukstadvaris. Clearly she was living in Aukstadvaris when she married Berka Pitum.

Although Berka Pitum was born in Stakliskes, he relocated to the nearby town of Aukstadvaris no later than the time of his marriage to Asnat. The wedding took place on March 13, 1914, when she was 24 and he was either 23 or 25 depending upon which birth date information is correct.

The marriage ceremony was performed by Rabbi Ruvin (Reuven) Braz (Baraz). It was witnessed by two men: Nesanel Keidanski and Iudel Zon (with "Zon" usually meaning "son of", in this case "son of Iudel"). Payment to the rabbi was 75 rubles, a standard fee for marriages at that time.

Rabbi Ruven Braz - date of photo unknown; lived approximately 1880 to 1961.

Source: www.myheritage.com (Braz family tree)

With respect to my grandmother, Asnat Baron, her parents were named Rachel Miller and Rael (Rachmil) Baron. One of Asnat's brothers was Julius Baron, who ultimately immigrated to the United States ahead of Feivel Pitum and sponsored Feivel's trip to the US and his immigration to his new country.

The children of the marriage of Berka and Asnat were Feivel, Leah and Rachel Feiga. Rachel Feiga was murdered near the end of 1940, ahead of her parents.

Leah managed to survive the killings and ultimately spent many years continuing to live in Lithuania under the Soviet Union's regime, finally immigrating to Israel in 1969, passing away in 1991 while living in Tel Aviv.

Both Berka and Asnat were murdered in Aukstadvaris in 1941, although a few months apart. The details are sketchy but my grandparents and my Aunt Rachel unfortunately became a part of the annihilation of Lithuanian Jewry.

Fourth Generation (Barry HALPERN)

Leah Pitum was married twice. Her first husband was Shtukarevich and he was killed during World War II. She was remarried in 1946 to a man named Lazkovich. Their marriage produced two children: Zalman, born in 1947 and Asia, born in 1952. Zalman and Asia are my first cousins, and none of us knew of the others' existence until Yom Kippur, 2009. As mentioned earlier, we "discovered" each other thanks to a then previously unknown third cousin of mine, Eden Joachim, who is a fellow researcher on Jewishgen.org.

Feivel Pitum, renamed Philip Halpern, married my mother, Minnie Waldman, on June 15, 1950. Their marriage produced one child, me – Barry Simon Halpern – born on November 23, 1952.

This photo is of Leah and young Zalman, dated late 1940s

Fifth Generation (Philip, Peter and Lisa HALPERN)

Barry Halpern married Ellen Zaslaw on December 24, 1972. Our marriage produced three children. Philip, born January 22, 1978; Peter, born October 5, 1979; Lisa, born February 9, 1982. Note that my son, Philip, carries the Hebrew/Yiddish names of his grandfather, Shraga Feivel.

Zalman Lazkovich married Ella Lenderman and their marriage produced two children: Anita, born 1978 and Lior, born 1982.

Asia Lazkovich married Misha Levit and their marriage produced two children: Anat, born 1982 and Guy, born 1985.

Zalman and Ella lived for many years in Toronto, Canada, though are in the process of relocating back to Israel, where their children both live. Asia and her family all live in Israel.

The Halpern family all lives in Colorado, with Barry and Ellen living in Boulder, and Philip, Peter and Lisa living in their own homes in Westminster.

THE THREE LIVES OF FEIVEL PITUM

- **1915 to 1934 – First Life: Feivel Pitum**

- **1934 to 1950 – Second Life: From Feivel to Philip**

- **1950 to 1966 – Third Life: Philip Halpern**

- **Feivel Pitum and Philip Halpern – an enduring life**

FEIVEL PITUM - HIS FIRST LIFE (1915 to 1934)

Feivel Pitum was born on July 19, 1915 in the Lithuanian shtetl (village) called Aukstadvaris. The town's name means "elevated estate", and was originally famous for being the home of some of Lithuania's well-known princes. The Russian and Yiddish names for the town are similar: Visokidvor. The town is close to Troki/Trakai (within 20 miles) and to the district's larger and better known central city of Vilnius (within 40 miles). Vilnius was known at the time as the "Jerusalem of the East" due to its rich Jewish cultural heritage and source of much Jewish learning, study and leadership. Members of the town were also active Zionists, as was true of Jews in other small towns in that area

Aukstadvaris was a small town containing perhaps no more than a few hundred Jewish people at its maximum, with a total population of perhaps 1,000 people. Just prior to the end of World War I in 1918, control of the town was passed between the Polish and Lithuanian armies.

The first Jews came to Aukstadvaris in the 1600's and possibly earlier. By 1925, the 65 Jewish families in town totalled 272 people. They were storekeepers, tailors, butchers, gardeners, and teachers. It is very possible that the Pitum family engaged in sewing and knitting in town, particularly given that there is evidence that those who immigrated to the United States were engaged in these types of occupations. Several families in town relied completely on the support of their families abroad. Over time, 55 of the families depended at least partially on support from abroad, with amounts ranging from $5 to $25 per month. There is evidence that Asnat's brother Julius Baron provided some type of support for his sister. By 1933, at least one source states that only 80 Jewish families remained in the town.[4]

The Rabbi in Aukstadvaris from 1900 to 1932 was

---

[4] Encyclopedia of Jewish Life Before and During the Holocaust. Ed. Shmuel Spector, and Geoffrey Wigoder. New York University Press, 2001

Rabbi Reuven Baraz; this is the rabbi who performed the marriage ceremony in 1914 between my grandparents Berka Pitum and Asnat Baron.

Rabbi Baraz had set up an elementary school in 1930. Speculating again, it is possible that Feivel's sisters, aged seven and ten at the time, may have attended this school. The Rabbi immigrated to Palestine (Israel) in 1932.[5] Could his departure have provided motivation for Feivel to leave Aukstadvaris eighteen months later? And why did Feivel emigrate to the US and not to Palestine? My own guess on this is that it was because he already had at least two uncles living in the United States, and they were probably suggesting to Feivel's parents that the US was the safer, more lucrative alternative at the time.

As mentioned previously, the Pitum family did not originate in Aukstadvaris, but came from the nearby town of Stoklishok (Stakliskes), fewer than 10 miles away. Feivel's mother's family, with the regal name of "Baron", apparently had been in Aukstadvaris for several generations, and I do not yet know where they originated.

As mentioned earlier, my grandparents were married in Aukstadvaris in 1914, and Feivel was born in 1915. The records show that two other Pitums were married in Stakliskes in the years 1898 and 1900, with the ceremonies performed by a Rabbi Elpern. Could this Rabbi have been a relative of mine, or is this just a coincidence? Samuel Halpern, Feivel's uncle, came to the US and retained the Halpern name, but as of this writing, I have (so far) no genealogical research results for this line of my family.

---

[5] Aukstadvaris chapter of Pinkas Hakehillot Lita, Dov Levin, translated by Shaul Yannai, 1966

The birth data that we have for Feivel's ancestors is of course uncertain, based mainly on the vital records of the town of Stakliskes. These records, when available, have been copied and translated, mainly by the Litvak Special Interest Group ("LitvakSIG"). What they tell us is that Feivel's Pitum ancestors all lived in the town during the various census dates. They tell us their ages, which give us their birth years, and they provide some family information. We can surmise that since there are no written histories of the Pitum family (that we know of) that they must have been a part of the "working class" of average man and woman. These ancestors of Feivel, my ancestors, all survived long enough to marry, to have children and to continue the Pitum line.

Where did the Pitums originally come from? For how long were they in Lithuania? When did they arrive in Stakliskes? Again, we can only guess based on general histories. Prior to 1795, the town was a part of the Polish-Lithuanian kingdom, and later became a part of Russia and the Russian Empire (in the early 1800's).

Jews first came to Stakliskes in the early 1700s, totalling about 500 by 1850, or about one-third of the total population. They were engaged in occupations such as fishing, agriculture, timber and even brewing beer. They had built a synagogue by the middle of the 19th century. By the 1870s a series of events initiated the departure of Jews from the town. These events included two major fires that destroyed many Jewish homes. Some people immigrated to Israel, while others moved elsewhere in Lithuania. [6]

By 1923, the town had about 1800 total residents, with 400 Jews, and by 1939 only 70 Jewish families were left in Stakliskes. We don't know how many of the Pitums remained behind, but it is likely that at least a few did. The Jews of Stakliskes were known for their support of the Zionist movement, and particularly for support of Zionist youth organizations. I can make a guess that young Feivel, with his

---

[6] www.shtetlinks.jewishgen.org - Stakliskes-Stoklishok written by Yosef Rosin, English edited by Sarah and Mordecai Kopfstein

father's contacts in Stakliskes, became involved in these groups through those contacts.

In terms of Feivel's childhood in Aukstadvaris, I have very few details. Below is a photo of Aukstadvaris during the 1930s. The building on the left in the front is Jewish elementary school, and the building behind it is the Beit Midrash or Hebrew religious school.

Aukstadvaris - 1930;
Photo courtesy Yad Vashem digital photo
archive 1131/139, submitter Dvora Kamzon

I know that Feivel attended school (from US naturalization records) for 14 of his 18 years in Aukstadvaris. I do remember that when I was a child, both of my parents emphasized to me how important education was, how important it was to study, and how important it would later be to attend a college or university, though neither of them had done so themselves. My mother had graduated from high school near the top of her class, and clearly my father had wished that his higher education had continued. However, I always knew that he was a voracious reader, with some of his books (mainly about history, Judaism, and Israel) still holding a place in my own library.

Feivel attended what he referred to in English as the

"University of Lithuania". According to Wikipedia, there is and was such a university, located in Kaunas (Kovno) which is about 50 miles from Aukstadvaris. That must have been quite a trip for Feivel to make and it's very likely he would have boarded in Kaunas during his university days. He likely would not have completed his university study however, as there is no evidence of an undergraduate degree. Here is the description of the school, from Wikipedia:

> *"Vytautas Magnus University (VMU) (Lithuanian: Vytauto Didžiojo Universitetas(VDU)) is a public university in Kaunas, Lithuania. The university was founded in 1922 during the interwar period as an alternate national university. Initially it was known as the **University of Lithuania**, but in 1930 the university was renamed to Vytautas Magnus University, commemorating 500 years of death of Vytautas the Great, the Lithuanian ruler, well known for the nation's greatest historical expansion in the 15th century."*

It makes sense that Feivel would still have listed this school as the "University of Lithuania" even though the name had been changed in 1930.

Feivel specialized in the study of history and geography, but did not learn any English until his later arrival in the United States.

In 1934, when he was only 18 years old, Feivel made the bold decision to leave Lithuania and journey to the United States. Preceding him was Asnat's brother Julius Baron, who had emigrated to the US in 1905, and must have advised his sister that Feivel would do better by leaving home, choosing the US and not Palestine (Israel). The climate for Jews was deteriorating in Eastern Europe and Lithuania, and must have been getting noticeably worse in Aukstadvaris and the Trakai district.

31

Feivel's permission to leave Lithuania

So after making appropriate applications for the required travel documents, Feivel set out for the voyage to his new world. At the time, he must have envisioned that he would see his family again in the future, either in the US or in Lithuania. Unfortunately, this was not to be. His farewell to his family in 1934 would be the last time he would see any of them. Could he have suspected that? Did they hug? Did they cry? How strong were the emotions on that day he said goodbye?

Feivel came to the US on the ship *"Britannic"*, which sailed from Liverpool to the port of Boston. The ship had three classes of travel: cabin, tourist and third class. Feivel travelled in third class (not a surprise given his limited funds and the fact that his voyage had been funded by his uncle, Julius Baron).

Postcard from the Britannic, 1934
From (Philip Halpern's travel wallet)

The *Britannic* (sailing under the "White Star" line, later Cunard) had been launched only a few years earlier and later became a troop transport ship during WWII, carrying more than 180,000 troops and travelling 376,000 miles. The ship carried a total of more than 1600 passengers in its three classes, with just over 600 travelling in "third class". The *Britannic* was more than 200 meters long, or well over 600 feet (two football fields).[7] But for Feivel, it was his home for the several days' voyage, and it must have seemed massive to him.

Some of the cabins slept only two persons, while most slept four. We can guess that Feivel likely had three roommates during his voyage, very possibly young men in similar situations. The ship appears to have made the Atlantic crossing about once every month during this time period.

---

[7] www.cunard.com

Leaving his small hometown of Aukstadvaris, Feivel had made what was probably his first journey through Europe, through Hamburg, across the English Channel and into Liverpool, setting sail on the *Britannic* in April of 1934, a few months short of his 19th birthday. In addition to leaving behind his family, there was also someone else who was special to him – Esther – about whom we will likely never know more. Clearly Esther meant a lot to him, as evidenced by the draft letter that he had written and saved during the voyage. Before his ship's departure, he had sent her a postcard during his brief stay in England.

Feivel found his first ocean voyage to be rocky and he was prone to motion sickness. He ate little – he was small framed to begin with, only 5'5" tall and weighing perhaps a bit more than 140 pounds (a few pounds of which he later lost while serving in the US Army). To this youngster, fresh out of Europe, what an experience this must have been for him! Quoting his own words:

> *"On a ship there are amazing things, in general everything here is made using the latest techniques. On the ship there is theater, movies, and anything you can imagine, you will find on the ship."*

He obviously wasn't totally averse to food and eating as he saved a menu from the ship, printed in German. Passengers had to pay for their food, at least those in third class. The menu promised "good food and relaxation" to enjoy during the trip.

He arrived in the US eager to get involved with groups that might be able to help stem the rising tide of anti-Semitism in Europe, and the physical dangers that they presented to those he cared most about. He also arrived with a passion for Zionism and for creating the State of Israel. In his draft letter written aboard the *Britannic*, he made references to the youth group he belonged to in Lithuania, the "Gordoniya". This group, formed in 1923 (or perhaps 1925 in Poland; the record is conflicted), had as its mission the "building up of the homeland, education of members in humanistic values, the creation of a

---

working nation, the renaissance of Hebrew culture, and self-labor (avodah azmit)."[8]

The movement's founder, Aaron David Gordon, was not known to be dogmatic. He favored principles typical of "humanistic creativity." His movement specifically targeted the lower classes of Jewish society, which certainly must have appealed to Feivel.

Clearly at the time of Feivel's journey to the US, he had been active in the Gordonia movement in Lithuania, supportive of its philosophy and principles, and eager to continue his activities upon arrival in the United States. While still living in Lithuania, in the summer of 1933 when he was 18 years old, he had *"labored in a field for the Land of Israel Youth Labor Movement"*. In fact, there is a photograph (below) of a Gordonia "summer camp" from July 1933, which took place in Stoklishok/Stakliskes. Did Feivel attend this camp? Did he meet Esther at this camp? Who is the boy on the far right in the photograph, sitting close to a girl? What I do know is that an enlargement of that boy (also below), taken from a high-resolution copy of that photograph, shows a young man who very strongly resembles Feivel Pitum. While I cannot be 100% certain of the identification, the resemblance is striking. The summer camp took place only eight months prior to his departure for the US, and in the town of his father's birth. For him to have become so passionate about the Gordonia there must have been some triggering experience. Therefore, it is entirely possible that this photograph represents his participation.

Unfortunately, the record ends here. The rest will remain a mystery. There is no further mention of the Gordonia organization in Philip's later writings, after his arrival in the US. However, it is clear that the movement shaped his views towards Israel and Jews around the world, and combined with the Holocaust, drove and energized his activities and passions for the remainder of his life.

---

[8] Article on Gordonia, www.jewishvirtuallibrary.org

Top: Stoklishok, 1933; Gordonia summer camp

Bottom: blowup from far right of group photo

Photo courtesy US Holocaust Memorial Museum Digital Archives (photo #21944), photo courtesy of Libbey Sansanowicz

FROM FEIVEL PITUM TO PHILIP HALPERN - HIS
SECOND LIFE (1934 to 1950)

Feivel Pitum, now Philip Halpern, arrived in his new hometown of Boston on April 29, 1934, fresh off the *Britannic* and probably with one primary contact, his Uncle Julius Baron. He may also have had contact with his Uncle Samuel Halpern (who lived in Western Massachusetts, at least 100 miles from Boston) but I don't have any record of that. Philip had no more than $12 in his pockets, which actually was a good bit of money at that time. He likely spoke little or no English, but only Yiddish, Hebrew, Lithuanian, and probably some Polish and German.

His first home in the United States would be with Uncle Julius at 21 James Street in the Brookline section of Boston. Julius had arrived in the US in 1905, became a naturalized citizen in 1911 and was working with his brother Harry at the Baron Dress Company on Washington Street in Boston.

As the "new" Philip Halpern passed through immigration, he left Feivel behind, other than to those family members who would not see him again. He became Philip Halpern. The Halpern name must have been taken from a previous family immigrant, probably Samuel Halpern. Why did he choose Halpern and not Baron, particularly as Julius was his sponsor? We'll likely never know for certain the answer to that. In the shtetls across Eastern Europe, the surname "Halpern" or some variation of that name was relatively common. The date of the actual name change is also not known though it must have happened quickly. His alien registration card in 1934 shows his name as "Philip Halpern". The *Britannic* manifest (see a copy of it in the Appendix) still lists him as "Feivel Pitum". What I take away from all of this is that my name was probably close to being "Barry Pitum" rather than "Barry Halpern."

37

Julius Baron, as with many Jewish immigrants, had set up a clothing and tailoring business in Boston with his brother Harry. Philip must have had regular contact with his Uncle Harry Baron, but I have little memory of Harry and no knowledge of their interactions. Philip was given his first job in the United States with Julius, as well as his first place to live, so that he could get on his feet in his new world.

At that time, and for years later, I know that Philip corresponded regularly with his family and friends back home, but his old life must have seemed to be fading quickly for him. His concern over the safety of his family and friends never faded through the years ahead, as can be seen in his numerous writings and activities. Unfortunately, any letters that he may have written and sent off no longer exist. Certainly anything that found its way back to his old home in Aukstadvaris would have been lost during the war. Any drafts he may have written - and as I've discovered, he liked to write and save drafts - no longer exist.

During his journey to the United States, he clearly intended to continue his activities with the Gordonia. In fact, his companions in Lithuania had specifically requested that he make contact with their Gordonia counterparts in the United States. He had written a letter to their group chapter in Baltimore, asking for contact information for the group's chapter in Boston. He was even bringing "materials" along with him to help "energize" the movement in the US. It's likely, however, that the realities of adjusting to a new country and learning a new language necessarily dampened his initial plans. Despite no apparent further direct involvement in an organized fashion, his passion for the mission of the Gordonia never faded, as evidenced by his writings later in life.

There is no specific record of Philip's activities during this period in the United States and in Boston. Did he continue to correspond with Esther? Did he encourage his family – his parents, his sisters – to join him in the US? I can speculate that he must have wanted his family to join him in the United States. After all, it was common for one family member to leave the shtetl, stay in contact with relatives back in Europe, and then bring family members over as funds permitted. Harry and Julius Baron came first. Samuel Halpern. Philip. For whatever reason, though, the rest of his family never came.

From at least 1934-1941 (until his induction into the army) he worked for the Baron Dress Company as a "purchasing agent". His work involved buying the materials required to make the dresses sold by the business. From his records, it's clear that this was his occupation both before and after his service in the military.

Philip did not become a US citizen until 1942, after he was already in the army. His naturalization ceremony took place in 1942 in Miami, Florida. I know that he loved being a US citizen. He was proud of it. I remember this vaguely from when I was a child, but I can see in his writings that he espoused all of the values that are inherent in the freedoms and ideals of the United States.

Philip was drafted into the US Army in March, 1941, like so many other young men who were waiting and hoping that the US would not have to join the fight in World War II. By that date, one of his younger sisters, Rachel, had already been murdered. She died on December 10, 1940 at the age of 17, but the circumstances of her death are unknown. According to her "page of testimony" from Yad Vashem, Rachel worked as a "saleswoman in a store".[9] Two people provided testimony on her behalf. One appeared to be a friend named Zelig Katz and the other was a "member of the community", Jacob Safirstein. This same Jacob Safirstein provided testimony for about 150 individuals who were murdered in Aukstadvaris and he later wrote (in 1951) a chapter for a Yizkor Book (i.e. a memorial book) about the annihilation of the Jews of Aukstadvaris[10]. A translation of this particular chapter can be found on the Jewishgen.org website. In all of Lithuania, it is

---

[9] www.yadvashem.org contains much of the "testimony" pages related to my family and referenced in this book. See the Appendix for samples.

[10] "Annihilation of the Jews of Aukstadvaris and of Trakai...", Jacob Sapirstein, from "Lite" ed by Sudarsky, Katzenelenbogen, Kissin, Kagan, New York: Jewish Cultural Society, 1951

---

estimated that 94% of Lithuanian Jews were murdered during the war, a greater percentage than any other Eastern European country.

At the time he entered the army, was Philip already aware that his sister was dead? Were letters still being exchanged with his parents or had the flow run dry? His parents were still alive at that point, but again, did he know? Whatever the case, by that date, he knew that the US had to enter the war, and that his involvement might play a small part in stopping the Germans and the Axis powers.

In the summer of 1941 Jewish persecution throughout Europe rapidly accelerated. In Lithuania (and elsewhere), widespread executions began in July (on the heels of smaller scale actions prior to that) and continued thereafter. On September 21 in Aukstadvaris, the Jews were locked up in the Lithuanian school, and later transferred to the old military barracks in Trakai and kept there for 10 days. On Yom Kippur eve (September 30, 1941), armed Lithuanians (not military, but civilians) murdered about 200 Jews from Aukstadvaris as well as others from surrounding areas. The personal property of these victims was then looted from their homes.[11]

Berka Pitum was one of those murdered that day. Asnat Baron was also murdered in 1941 but the details are not known other than that they both probably died in Trakai. Again, Jacob Safirstein provided the Yad Vashem testimony.

Asnat's mother's maiden name was Rachel Miller (Baron was the paternal side of her family), and as mentioned earlier, was also from Aukstadvaris. During the Yom Kippur massacre in 1941 in Aukstadvaris, one Jewish person managed to call out before he was murdered. He screamed out and called for the avenging of the spilling of the blood. That man's name was Asher Miller. Was he my relative? I don't know. And it really doesn't matter. He was brave enough to scream

---

[11] "Aukstadvaris" chapter from Pinkas Hakehillot Lita, Dov Levin, Jerusalem, 1966 and "Annihilation of the Jews" chapter from Lite by Sapirstein

out against the injustice of that day and so many other days, and he spoke for all of our families, our mothers and fathers, brothers and sisters, cousins and neighbors.

Philip's sister, Leah Pitum, was aged 20 at the time of these massacres. She somehow survived the murders, went on to live in Lithuania under Soviet rule, and later immigrated to Israel. Her story has not yet been told in depth, but suffice it to say that she married twice and left two children, a son and daughter, who are my first cousins, Philip's/Feivel's niece and nephew. He never met them but knew of them through letters with his sister.

I don't know when Philip found out what happened to his family. How did he mourn? Who mourned with him? Like so many other questions, these will remain unanswered.

When Philip was drafted, he left his job with the Baron Dress Company to report for basic training at Camp Edwards on Cape Cod. Just prior to his being drafted, he was still living in Brookline, though had moved out of Uncle Julius's home. His service in the army began in the 26th infantry division at Camp Edwards on Cape Cod. As he arrived at Camp Edwards that day in March, 1941, he heard the band playing "You're in the Army Now!" Within days of his arrival there, he quickly made several friends, one of whom was Isadore ("Iz") Zack. Isadore later became a leader within the Anti Defamation League and served as a lifelong advocate for civil rights for all. During the war, he served in leadership roles in military intelligence. He would also deliver the memorial speech at Phil's Jeremiah Lodge memorial service in 1966, and it was clear that the two army buddies shared a common geopolitical worldview. He said about Philip:

> *"Phil Halpern knew why we fight...Phil knew the score...Phil knew why we were there...He never doubted the reasons for being in the military and getting ready to fight for ourselves and our families...Phil was passionate about the goals of the Anti Defamation League...He was the ideal ADL secret weapon!"*

The army was filling out the 104th infantry regiment and Phil and several of his new army buddies landed there. Company M, Phil's company, specialized in machine guns and mortars. The third battalion of the 104th infantry had a so-called "elite" group of 28 men who ran the battalion at Camp Edwards. Soon after Phil's and Iz's arrival, the army needed to select eight men to fill out a complement of 28 total. So they tested all of the new arrivals using the army's IQ tests, and chose the top eight. Phil was one. Iz was another. Of the eight chosen, four were Jewish. Phil was the only one in the group who had any kind of accent, and therefore the only one who was "new" to the US. Phil's many hours of night classes at Brookline High School (near Boston) to learn English certainly contributed to his mastery of the English language at such a high level (as evidenced by his success with the English-language IQ test) within seven years of his arrival in the United States.

Clearly Phil was welcomed and accepted within his group of army friends. One story from that time is illustrative.

Early in basic training, each week one of his friends would go home (most of them lived in the Boston area) and return to camp with a package of home-baked goods of some type: a box of strudel, scones, or other local favorite. Phil was a bit upset about this because he didn't have a real family at home in the Boston area. But he did have his Uncle Julius, and secretly asked Julius to prepare something for him that he could share with the guys. So a large package arrived for Phil, and his friends gathered round as he opened the package. Out came a home-baked Jewish rye bread. Next was a large, foot long kosher salami. And finally, a "Pinch Bottle" of Haig and Haig scotch! Alcohol was prohibited in boot camp but the men all managed to keep it a secret and ensure that its contents did not survive for long. In the eyes of his friends, Phil had contributed more than his share to army morale. I now like to think that my own love of scotch was passed from my father to me, though my childhood memory is that my father only drank Canadian Club whiskey.

During his basic training commitment, Phil earned his

nickname: "Casey". The origin of the name is lost in history. Was it KC? Did it somehow come from baseball and "Casey at the Bat"? Or was it related to some army activity and acronym? In any event, the only people who knew that nickname and the only people who ever used it were his army buddies. As a child, I had never heard that name being used.

Phil was very well liked and respected. He was neat and very "soldierly"; very proper. Not only his ability as an immigrant to fit in with the others, but his light-hearted manner, his sense of humor, all contributed to his ability to befriend others.

Basic training normally lasted about 14 weeks. At that time, before the US official entry into World War II, training was everything. Some men believed that the US would never enter the war and were hoping to obtain an early release. Iz was one of those people hoping for an early release - he was a few years older than the others and he was hoping that would earn him a discharge. However, December 7, 1941 (the Japanese bombing of Pearl Harbor and the official US entry into World War II) intervened and Phil and his buddies all remained in the service until 1945.

Phil was one of those chosen for a variety of various training programs. One was called the "Army Specialized Training Program" or ASTP. His background and strength in language, his experience in living in Europe, all of this made him a strong candidate for specialized training and future advancement.

He served in Company M, the 157th infantry regiment (as well as the 104th infantry upon his initial service). He received training in sharpshooting and apparently served in some type of military intelligence function, probably as a translator. Towards the end of his service, towards the end of the war in Europe, he served in the Rhineland and in Central Europe. He learned and became proficient in Morse Code, serving as a radio telegrapher, sending and receiving messages. Upon my "re-discovery" of his Morse Code proficiency and training records during my search for his history, I recalled that when I was a child he taught me Morse Code (which I have long since forgotten). We used to practice sending messages using a "straight key", a machine that created the buzzing long and short components (dots and dashes) that made up the code. I couldn't have been ten years old at the time. And I had never known why he was so proficient at that means of communication until I discovered more about his army service.

Through training in Maryland at Camp Ritchie, he learned how to interpret aerial photographs, which again helped him to engage more in military intelligence throughout his service career. As a result of his service, he received several awards: Medals for Good Conduct and for American Defense Service. He was awarded a ribbon for the European African Middle Eastern Theater Campaign.

Virtually all of his training and service occurred in the United States, until October, 1944 when thousands of men were transferred to the European theater for combat. All of the training that Phil and others had received was thrown out in exchange for the soldiers needed on the ground to fight the war. Phil spent about a year or so in Europe and was part of a forward regiment that chased the German army back to Austria. His role was to load the mortar shells. The resulting constant explosions left him with a lifelong impairment in hearing.

On the personal side, in 1941 Iz would take Phil home with him to meet his family so that he'd feel that he had a home. They would go out on dates together, with Iz seeing the woman who eventually would become his wife, Ruth Bennett, and Phil dating a woman named Libby. The first photo on the next page is of Phil and Ruth Bennett (later Ruth Zack) and her nephews at Iz's home in Massachusetts. The bottom photo is Phil with some of his army buddies.

Top: 1941 Phil with Ruth Bennet (Zack) and her nephews

Bottom: Phil with his army unit in 1941 (Phil is on the far left)

Because my father died so young and because I was so young when he died, we never had a chance to talk about his war service. The only thing I had ever heard about his time in the service was that he suffered a partial loss of hearing due to his being near a bomb when it exploded. I never knew he was in combat. I had been told that his hearing problem was due to an "accident" that didn't appear to be related to combat. Isadore Zack told me a different story, though. I never knew he received any awards or commendations. I never knew he was involved in military intelligence. My recent search and discovery have told me the story he was never able to do.

He received his honorable discharge and returned to his apartment in Brookline in November, 1945. Surely by this time he must have known of the death of his parents and his sister. He must have known of the survival of one sister, Leah, and was clearly anxious to see her again. Sadly, that would never happen, though the two of them were fortunate to be able to exchange a series of letters during the 1950s and 1960s.

The only insight into his personal life is a photograph I have of him in uniform in October 1945, together with a woman named Louise. They are dining at the Vienna Café in New York City, and celebrating some type of anniversary for the two of them, according to Louise's handwritten note on the back of the photo. Since Philip had been overseas during the war, I can guess that they must have known each other for more than a year or two or three.

Phil and Louise celebrating an "anniversary" in October 1945

There is no further record of Louise, nor of any other woman he dated.

Following his discharge, he resumed his working career with Julius Baron and the clothing business. By the time he and my mother married, or shortly thereafter, he must have entered the business that he would engage in for the remainder of his life: laundry and dry cleaning.

Once again, there are gaps in Philip's life history from his 1945 exit from military service until his June 1950 marriage to my mother Minnie Waldman.

Phil and Minnie circa 1950

PHILIP HALPERN - HIS THIRD LIFE (1950 to 1966)

Philip married my mother on June 15, 1950 and they began their married life in Dorchester, Massachusetts. I was born on November 23, 1952. I don't have details about their meeting and courtship. Both were 35 years old at the time of their marriage, which at that time made for a relatively "later in life" marriage. I recall (and I have some photos) that the wedding took place at the home of my mother's sister Sylvia (Waldman) Dobis in Wellesley. Sylvia and Joe Dobis's home was a mansion. When I was a child and we went to visit I was always in awe of this house and the grounds surrounding it! They were the owners of the Wellesley Hills Market which for many, many years was a well-known institution in Wellesley. Their home must have been a wonderful location for a wedding.

June 15, 1950 - wedding day

We lived in Dorchester until 1962, in two different homes that were close to each other. One was on Bradshaw Street, and the other was the Waldman family "homestead" at 80 Esmond Street. For my first few school years, I attended the Sarah Greenwood Elementary School, and it was close enough for me to walk to school every day. Esmond Street was in some ways a Jewish "ghetto" - working class Jewish families surrounded by other immigrant families. Our next-door neighbors were Holocaust survivors and came out of

49

concentration camps; I recall that at least one of them had numbers tattooed on their arms. Down the street from our house was the Esmond Street Church, where my friends and I would go inside after school to visit the nuns, who I recall as showing only kindness to the neighborhood children, black and white, Jewish and Catholic.

My father would make the drive from Dorchester to Nantasket Beach (in the town of Hull) every day of the week. I remember him in the winter having to shovel out from blizzards. I remember him in the fall having to drive in the midst of hurricane warnings and occasionally an actual hurricane.

For at least a year prior to our living on Esmond Street we did live in Hull full time. It was before I started going to school, and we rented a home on Lynn Avenue. In other years we would spend our summers at Nantasket Beach, usually staying in a cottage owned by my Aunt Leah (my mother's sister). For my father it was the busiest time of year for the Surfside Laundromat and it was also nice for us all to have the beach and ocean nearby. His laundries were not always "coin-operated". Initially his business on Nantasket Avenue was a drop off and pickup operation. The machines were in the back and I would climb up on the shelves and peek out through the opening, watching my father at work in the front of the shop.

At some point, he got rid of that original business and opened the automated place across the street from there. It started as a laundry business and then he rented more space and expanded to an automated dry cleaning operation. I helped whenever I could, particularly during the summers, and I actually learned quite a bit about how all those machines worked, and how to repair them when they didn't. I enjoyed climbing up on top of a malfunctioning machine, hanging over the back of it and trying to see whether it was a belt or a solenoid that wasn't working properly. After my father died, my familiarity with the workings of the machines helped my mother and me to keep the business running for the year or so until we sold it.

My memories of those summers are filled with my

father and I having a catch in the yard by ourselves, or that he finally had some time to play ball with my cousins, my friends and me. Even though he had to work a lot in the summer, at least he didn't have to do the daily drives so he had more time at home. If I recall correctly, I think he had help with the Framingham location so that he didn't have to do those drives so often in the summers.

My memories are fuzzy when it comes to what the laundromats actually looked like. These old photographs are the only ones I have.

Top: Surfside Laundromat on Nantasket Avenue

Bottom: The dry cleaning half of the business

No family history of Philip would be complete without at least a passing mention of another passion of his that was passed on to me, and to my children. Baseball and the Boston Red Sox. I don't know when the new immigrant Feivel learned to love baseball and the Red Sox. I do know that one of my earliest childhood memories (probably 1956-57) are of my father and me together, walking up the first base ramp to our seats inside Fenway Park, and being dazzled by the green – the green monster, the green grass, the green walls. One of the earliest home movies I have is of my father and me walking into a room at home, carrying a Red Sox pennant, which is an anachronism since the Sox of the 1950s were truly a terrible team. It wasn't until 1967, or two seasons after my father's death, that the Sox finally won the American League Pennant.

My father had seen the Sox win a pennant in 1946, though he never got to see them win the World Series. He arrived in the US in 1934 and surely knew nothing about baseball. Soccer, yes. Baseball, no. What drew him to baseball? I have my own theory on this. It was in 1934 that the Detroit Tigers won the American League pennant for the first time in many, many years. The first American Jewish superstar athlete, Hank Greenberg, led that team. Greenberg created a stir during the pennant race in September by announcing that he would not play on either Rosh Hashanah or Yom Kippur. After consultation with his rabbi, he wound up playing on Rosh Hashanah, the Jewish New Year, but did not play on Yom Kippur, the holiest date on the Jewish Calendar. This debate involving Greenberg received much public attention, particularly amongst the Jewish American community. My father, only in the US for a few months when the Greenberg discussion was occurring, surely must have taken note of it. In fact, Detroit was due to play the Boston Red Sox on September 10, 1934, Rosh Hashanah, in Detroit. Perhaps Philip felt that if a young Jewish kid, only a few years older than himself (Greenberg was born in 1911), could be so successful and so prominent in the American pastime, then this "baseball" sport was something he should pay some attention to. As I said, this is speculation on my part, but the story does fit, and from my interactions with my father, it seemed as though he had been passionate about baseball for his whole life. It turned out that on that Rosh Hashanah game, Greenberg hit two homes runs to lead the Tigers to victory over the Red Sox.

I'm sure my father would be gratified that his love and passion for the Red Sox remains alive in his grandchildren.

Phil and Barry and the Red Sox

Moving to Milton in 1962, I began my schooling at Tucker Elementary School, across from the second floor apartment we were renting at 200 Blue Hills Parkway. This would be my father's last residence, and sadly he never actually owned a home. At some point after we moved to Milton, he opened his second laundry business, in Framingham, which made the daily drive and the long hours both even longer.

We kept a kosher home throughout our time in Dorchester, Nantasket and Milton. We had two sets of dishes for dairy and for meat, and two more sets of dishes for Passover. I figured out later that we actually had a fifth set of dishes for "*traif*" or non-kosher food (mostly for Chinese take out). My father was generally observant. He went to *shul* whenever he could and always on the high holidays. In Milton we belonged to a conservative temple, Temple Shalom on Blue Hill Avenue, which is where I went to Hebrew School, where I became a Bar Mitzvah in 1965, and later was the site of my wedding in 1972. My father also would walk to the orthodox *shul*, B'nai Jacob, where he would frequently go with some of

---

53

my uncles.

I know that my father valued Jewish traditions and that's why he kept a kosher home. But he also valued other things about his home in America. He loved lobster. Not kosher. He would often take me out to breakfast on Sunday mornings and we would have French toast and sausage. Pork sausage. And of course he loved Chinese food, and pork fried rice. So while the traditions were important, he had his priorities!

When I was growing up, he was strict. Or at least he seemed strict. On the other hand, not a day went by without him telling me that he loved me. Every day, multiple times a day. That has always stuck with me. I was never "afraid" of him even when I did something wrong. I knew he would support me no matter what, and I knew that he would teach me whatever needed to be taught.

I do remember a few vignettes from over the years, with memory foggy in time, but the images have stayed with me. He and my mother would often take me to Franklin Park Zoo. We would go into Boston and ride the swan boats. We would go to baseball games. How my father had time for this, I really can't remember, because it also seemed as though he was always working.

One incident I remember, I must have been six or seven and we were living at that time on Bradshaw Street. We had taken a walk to the zoo and were coming back but he had forgotten his keys. The doorbell didn't work and my mother didn't know we were out there. So we stood outside, picked up some stones and started throwing them at the different windows, hoping that my mother would hear us. She finally did. It was the stone that broke the window that did it. I thought my father would be furious, but he laughed so hard when it happened!

Another memory: He wanted me to fly on an airplane, and take a train. So we spent one day (I think it was one day), taking a train to New York City, and then a plane home. I don't remember much at all about that day in New York. But I do

---

remember that my father wanted to spend the day travelling with me. I know that we went to the World's Fair in New York together, but I'm not sure whether it was this time we took the plane and train, or another time.

We would take other drives together as a family, sometimes with a cousin, usually my cousin Stanley. My father would drive, always speeding, always trying to catch the car in front of him. He loved to drive. I know that he got caught speeding more than once and frequently seemed to talk his way out of it. On the long drives we took together, he would sing, though these were not songs that anyone else had ever heard. The most memorable song was "I got a hole in my pants". I clearly remember that song more than any other. The lyrics went something like this:

"I got a hole in my pants...

I got a hole in my pants..."

I don't believe that this tune was a hit, other than in our own car, and I think that even this is an over-statement.

That song was evidence of his sense of humor. He loved to laugh. He had a smile that made you smile and it shows through in the photographs of him. He could be very serious, but he also recognized that people had to lighten up a little at times.

We also drove to Montreal a few times. My godmother Helen Wener, a Canadian, was a friend of my mother's, and we would drive up and back to visit her for a long weekend.

Philip was a smoker. He constantly had a cigarette in his mouth or his hand. His brand was Camels, three packs a day. This could not have been good for his heart, though he was never diagnosed with any serious medical issues until the day he died.

As mentioned earlier, Philip was heavily active in various Jewish volunteer organizations that were associated with the B'nai B'rith. As I think back, it amazes me he had so much time for his family and for his passions, in addition to his businesses.

One of the organizations he was involved with was the Jeremiah Lodge, the men's group of B'nai B'rith. In one of its 1963 newsletters, there was a "profile" of Philip:

> *"B'nai B'rith was a way of life to Phil long before he joined Jeremiah Lodge. He is a past Vice President of Blue Hills Lodge and served, strangely enough, as its ADL Chairman. On several occasions he has served ADL on classified missions and he has received Special Citations for Outstanding Service from the New England Regional Office and from the District Grand Lodge. Phil has brought to us a conviction and devotion quite apart from the usual. He does not mouth the words of others; he does not regard his chairmanship as a task. He seeks out the truth, and through work and thought he has brought a new image of ADL to us. His words both written and oral have, of late, been somewhat prophetic.*
>
> *Along with his love and work for B'nai B'rith, Phil is intensely interested in ORT, the Organization for Rehabilitation through Training, which has brought hope for a new life to countless displaced Jews. It is only fitting, perhaps, that such a man as Phil has devoted himself to the plight of others, when all that he has achieved has been through his own struggle.*
>
> *As always, it is somewhat presumptuous to even "profile" that which is a man. That which may be most indicative of Phil Halpern has been said in words far beyond my limited range. As it is said in the Book of Proverbs:*
>
> *"Intelligence is a source of life unto its possessor. The heart of the wise maketh its*

---

mouth intelligent. And upon his lips, he increaseth information."

It is not clear who wrote this profile. When I read it, and also read his own contemporaneous editorials, I was struck by the fact that they were somewhat prophetic. I was pleased to see that at least some people recognized this in him while he was still alive.

Philip remained very involved with his wartime friend Iz (Isadore) Zack until his death and perhaps it was Iz who either wrote or contributed to that profile.

What Philip did for his various organizations is difficult to reconstruct so many years after his passing. What he wrote and what he thought at the time, however, is available to some extent. He wrote editorials for the newsletter of Jeremiah Lodge. I've selected a couple of them to excerpt, as I believe they represent his life's thinking as well as his life's teaching to others.

His topics, while relevant to his time, also resonate today. In one article opining about the "Nation of Islam" or "Black Muslims", he was expressing concerns about the philosophies and rise of the "Nation of Islam", while at the same time expressing knowledge and wisdom with respect to Islam itself:

> *"The question of how "Moslem" the "Muslims" are is not clear at all. As a matter of fact Muslim Racism clearly flaunts the basic Moslem doctrine that all men, regardless of color, are brothers."*

I wonder what he would be saying today. My guess is that he would still hold true to his values and beliefs from the 1960s, and in this one example I have learned so much of how my views, ideals and beliefs have been formed.

In another article about anti-Semitism and the Roman Catholic Church, he spoke of the roots of anti-Semitism and the need for reform in actions and attitudes. He was not afraid to raise controversial topics or to espouse views from his lifelong

—

beliefs:

> *"The church should have the courage to insist that the teaching of this period be reformed so as to ensure a proper historical perspective on the one hand, and to fight the traditional doctrine whereby contemporary Jews are identified with the Jews depicted in the final scenes of the Gospels.*
>
> *The anti-Jewish myth created by these teachings has been the most malignant root of Western anti-Semitism.*
>
> *It is more relevant to question their relationship to the destruction of Europe's Jews, than the part played by the silence of Pope Pius XII during the Nazi era."*

I wrote earlier about my quest to learn more about my father, who he was, what he thought, and what of him still lives within me. Perhaps that is best exemplified by one more example of his writings (which is reprinted in full in the appendix). When I shared this with my children, my daughter Lisa came back to me and said: *"He was writing to us."* That is, my father Philip was writing to my children, to his grandchildren and to their own grandchildren. The startling fact is that he was writing this while I was not yet a teenager...His topic for that article was nothing less than the survival of the Jewish people and our heritage, through education. His words are no less relevant today than they were almost fifty years ago when he wrote them:

> *"One of the principal causes for the survival of the Jewish people throughout the ages is our Culture and Heritage.*
>
> *In our time, however, study on the part of Adult Jews has been neglected or shall we say an "I don't care" attitude has evolved. Most Jews today are pathetically uninformed in the matter of Jewish culture...and, if possible, his children know less.*

The adult Jew presents a strange paradox to the world...a man who knows all literature except his own...all philosophies but that of his own people.

We read books in twenty-nine tongues but we generally cannot understand a word of Hebrew.

We have plenty of time, it seems, to watch "The Defenders" on TV but have no time to learn about the "Defenders" of our own heritage.

We build structures of steel and stone but fail to build the minds of Jewish men. We devote our efforts to the education of our children, but fail to realize that the child honors only the ideals and practices of his parents.

Deeper concepts must be understood by mature men before they can be transmitted to the oncoming generations. The failure is all the more serious in the light of the challenges now confronting Judaism and the Jewish way of life.

In the determining of our future, the development of knowledgeable Jews is vital and could well prove decisive.

The world will be the loser if the Jewish traditions and culture vanishes, for in that event, there will have been eliminated from the human spirit a unique and irreplaceable color which has lent so much and has so much more to lend to the beauty of the world."

Throughout the post-war years, he corresponded regularly with his sister Leah, still living in Lithuania as a part of the Soviet Union. While letters to and from each other would normally have been censored, the letters that he saved appear to have escaped the censors. Perhaps they were too "routine" to attract attention. One letter was written in late 1965, around the time of my bar mitzvah. Leah refers in the letter to her happiness about the bar mitzvah. She writes of

Uncle Julius, referring to him as "Uncle Joshua". She is eager to hear from brother Feivel about the details of the bar mitzvah.

She refers to her sister-in-law, her husband's sister, and the fact that they had immigrated to Israel within the past two years (approximately 1963). Leah's husband works and her two children (whom I later learned to be Zalman and Asia) attend school. She is happy to hear that Feivel continues to attend *shul* and pray.

In closing this particular letter, Leah expresses her "wish we should live to see each other." Very sadly, that was not to be.

FEIVEL PITUM AND PHILIP HALPERN - HIS ENDURING LIFE

In the year 2005, I created a book as a birthday gift for my mother Minnie's 90th birthday. It was a collection of my writings that began generally when we relocated from Connecticut to Hong Kong in 1990. I titled the book *"Once You Leave Home"*. The phrase came from some advice I had been given just prior to the start of my journey from the US to live and work in Asia for the next eighteen years. The full message of the quotation was "once you leave home, you can never go back".

Certainly this was true of Feivel Pitum. When he journeyed from Lithuania in 1934, he left behind one world for another. He clearly couldn't go back because the world he left behind had ceased to exist (certainly more literally than my world of 1990 ceased to exist for me.) However, as he learned throughout the 32 years of his adult life in the United States, while you couldn't go back home, you could retain very important facets of your old life – those that ground you. For him, this was made up of two parts: first, his Jewish culture and heritage that had survived and been passed on through generations, and that shaped his world view; and second, his family - his family in the United States and his family on the other side of the world, all of whom meant everything to him and drove his quest to make a better world for them and their children.

When my father passed those four quarters to me on that Sunday in 1966, he had a look in his eyes that struck me at the time - I've later described it in one word as "sadness", though I've never thought that did justice to what I saw in his eyes. It turned out that this would be the final time that he would pass a few coins my way, and the final time that we had a chance to share a private moment. Could he have known? Could he have sensed that something was physically wrong with him, but not enough to raise that sense to a conscious level? Maybe. Maybe not.

—

What I know is that he had so much he wanted to tell me and to teach me, and sadly, there was not enough time remaining to do that.

Only years later, as I learned bits and pieces about his and my family's history, did I know enough to fully comprehend his message to me that day, that final day that changed my life. Whether his message was intended on a conscious level (I doubt it) or whether it's something I've simply put my own spin on, I know this: He wanted me to understand where he came from, what shaped his thoughts and what purpose he had in life. By better understanding him, so many years after his death, I have gained great insights into my own life, my own history, my path towards the future, and what I want to leave for my children and for their children.

Why must we all learn where we come from?

Why must we all learn what made us the way we are? For our children? Certainly. For their children? Absolutely. For ourselves? Most importantly, because it is only "ourselves" who we can shape with absolute certainty.

When I read and re-read some of my father's writings, whether he was writing on the *Britannic* as a naïve young

—

eighteen year old, or as a more mature adult, I see some of myself and what I have become. He could not possibly have taught that to me – he didn't have the time or the opportunity. In the look he gave me that day, he passed something of himself to me. It was a message of "never forget: learn as much of the lessons of the past as you can, and become the very best person that you can be."

"The world will be the loser if the Jewish traditions and culture vanishes, for in that event, there will have been eliminated from the human spirit a unique and irreplaceable color which has lent so much and has so much more to lend to the beauty of the world."

Feivel Pitum as Philip Halpern

ACKNOWLEDGEMENTS

So many people have inspired me with my research and my commitment to writing this book. If I don't mention you by name here, it's not because I haven't appreciated your help and inspiration. It's much more likely that I carelessly omitted writing you in. Please forgive me.

I want to first thank Eden Joachim whose work on Jewishgen and the Pitum family is what really jump-started my journey into the discovery of my father's past. Zalman Lazkovich provided my flesh and blood link to my flesh and blood. David Kanter showed me that genealogy is really a science requiring rigorous thought, organization and documentation. Isadore Zack was gracious enough to spend a couple of hours with me and share his memories of my father. Shai Kowitt and Jack Welner provided important translations of my father's letters. My friends at the Jewish Genealogical Society of Colorado have provided continued education and motivation, not to mention that their expertise continues to make me realize I still have a lot to learn. My Irish-led genealogical friends from the Boulder and Louisville, Colorado area have been enormously motivational to me, helping with ideas and solutions to my research – you know who you are! My fellow author Alan Bourey provided some wonderful guidance on actually getting a book finished and ready to publish.

There are a number of photographs throughout the book and most of them are my own, taken by my father, mother, me or a relative or friend. A few photographs come from outside sources, namely online web sites which are a wonderful resource. For each of those photos, I have done my best to give appropriate and accurate credit, and for each I have attempted to or obtained permission from the owners of the photos. If I've mistakenly identified any of them, I will correct that oversight in the next edition of the book. I continue to appreciate the efforts undertaken by so many across the world to provide public access to a wealth of information and resources that makes all of our genealogical journeys so much more fruitful.

—

An early manuscript of this book was given to each of my children – Philip, Peter and Lisa - and I appreciate their comments and input. I need to thank my mother, not just for her lifelong confidence in me, but also for having the foresight to save so much of my father's things knowing that one day I would actually take some interest in them! My faithful dog Linea has spent many hours at my feet providing support in her own special way, and never complained a bit. Finally, my wife Ellen has supported me throughout, particularly on those long days when I disappeared into my basement work area, seemingly never to surface. Without her, my lifelong best friend, motivator and inspirer, I would never have been able to do any of this.

APPENDICES

1. The Pitum Family – A Conjectural History
2. Timeline/Key Events in Life of Philip Halpern
3. Sample writings of Philip Halpern
   Adult Jewish Education – April, 1963
   There is no "Negro Problem
   As I See It – 1964
   It's Amazing
   Passover Thoughts
   JFK Tribute – 1963
   "The Bible and the Twist"
   A Controversial Play – 1964
   A Jew Looks Toward the Ecumenical Council - 1963
   Editorial Regarding Black Muslims – 1964
   Miscellaneous notes and Correspondence
4. Isadore Zack – a brief biography
5. Anti Defamation League speakers – a selection
   a.   Ephraim Isaac – Ethiopian Jewry – 1964
   b.   David Chajmowixz – Cuban Jewry – 1964
   c.   Pho Ba Hai – Vietnamese – 1965
   d.   Haskell Kassler – civil rights attorney – 1958
6. Pedigree chart for Feivel Pitum - conjectural
7. Miscellaneous documents and maps
8. Sources and Bibliography

THE PITUM FAMILY HISTORY

Generation by Generation – A Conjectural History

As I described in the main text, I believe that the following is my Pitum family history, based on the "preponderance of the evidence", to use a legal term. However, I can't prove it, and if it can't be proved, then I can't present it as fact. So the following genealogy is conjectural. It's a conjecture of what "might have been" or what may be true. There are eight generations presented, which contain five generations about which I am certain and which are contained in the main text of the book. The additional three generations are the ones for which I have doubts.

Let me begin by describing the area of uncertainty in my historical tracing. This will show how difficult it is to find accurate records, to read them, to translate them, and to ensure that they are accurately understood.

In the fourth generation below, my father's grandfather (my own great-grandfather) is named Arie Leib Pitum. Of that we are certain (the names were passed down by my father's sister Leah), though there may be variations in how the spelling of the names is presented. The English translation of the Lithuanian 1858 Revision List for Stakliskes shows an "Aron Pitum", son of Beniamin and Sara. So, unless "Arie Lieb" is the same person as "Aron" then the backwards tracing fails.

Why do I think that Arie and Aron are the same person? The two names are definitely not the same name; that is, they are not simply two different spellings of the same name. They are totally different names and if they are indeed accurately presented, then they represent two entirely different Pitums.

In English the letters aren't all that different, but the original language was not English. I have examined a copy of the original record from which the translation was made. The original language was Lithuanian Cyrillic. In reading the letters of the name as written, I can make out something like "A-R-O-N-E", though I can't be certain of that because of the scribbles in the document. Normally an "E" is not appended to a written

---

name such as "Aron." Further, if the name SHOULD have been written as "A-R-I-E" then it wouldn't have taken much to write the name differently – only one letter and in the Cyrillic they are not that different in appearance.

My research into the names of people living in Stakliskes in the 1800s shows names of several Pitum families. Of these, the ones contained in my conjectural history below are the only Pitums who could possibly be my father's ancestors. The other names of the other Pitums do not match. Of course, perhaps for some reason my Pitum ancestors weren't recorded. Perhaps they weren't recorded in the Stakliskes records, but would show up in some other town's records. Perhaps they weren't recorded at all.

In addition, one of the family members, or his son, was likely a witness at the wedding of my father's father, according to the names of the witnesses listed on the marriage information I obtained from original Lithuanian records.

Further, my father's grandfather, Arie Leib, could have been named after his own (i.e. Arie Leib's) grandfather, whose name is recorded as "Leyba" (though this was a very common name at that time, so this could simply be a coincidence).

For the above reasons, given the data that I have to work with, my own conclusion is that these are "my" Pitums.

What if I'm wrong? What if Aron is not Arie?

First, I have to conclude that I'll likely never get the true tracing because as I said, I have found no other alternative families who might fit. Second and perhaps even more important, even if these are NOT my father's direct ancestors, they are likely to be relatives – probably cousins. Further, my actual Pitum ancestors would have had similar names, similar homes, and similar histories. So, in the event I do not achieve 100% certainty (or even 80% certainty), I know that my ancestors lived similar lives to the people I've listed here.

Therefore, with all of the above in mind, I present my "conjectural" generation by generation Pitum family history...Please note that some of what follows below is

—

repetitive with the main text, though I have not included any of the maps or photos that have already been presented.

First generation (Abram PITUM):

Abram (Avraham) PITUM was born probably around 1760, in the small Lithuanian town of Stakliskes (Yiddish), also known as Stoklishok (Lithuanian). Lithuania's history is one of changing borders and governments, at one time independent, then under Poland or Russia, and then independent again. Names and spellings of towns depend upon sources, which could be Yiddish, Lithuanian, or Russian.

Stakliskes is located within the Troki (Trakai) and Vilnius (Vilna) district (or "guberniya") depending upon the timeframe. The town had a Jewish population that approached 1,000 by the year 1900, and at various times comprised 30-40% of the total population.

I know virtually nothing about Abram Pitum as no family records exist from that time.

Second generation (Leyba PITUM):

Abram Pitum had two sons, Leyba and Girsha. Leyba was born in 1786; I know this from the vital records (also referred to as census) information that is available. Girsha's birth year is unknown. Based on what is known about Leyba, I've made a rough guess as to his father Abram's birth year (i.e. 1760s).

In the census information (in this case, the so-called 1858 "revision list"), Lebya's surname is listed as both Pitum and Tarvod. Given that there is no other relevant information, I might guess that Tarvod could have been his mother's maiden name. It was common for the surname to be passed down from the mother rather than the father, although it was the Pitum name that eventually survived. In any event, research thus far has failed to provide any further information on the name "Tarvod".

Leyba married Beila, who was born in 1788 and was thus two years younger than her husband.

74

Girsha also was married, though there is no further information about his wife.

Third generation (Beniamin PITUM):

Leyba and Beila had two sons: Beniamin (Benjamin) and Itsko. Beniamin was born in 1813, when his father and mother were 27 and 25 years old respectively. Itsko was born several years later, in 1819, when his parents were a relatively older 33 and 31.

Beniamin married Sora, four years younger than he was. Itsko married Chaya Dverka, only one year younger. There is no information about the women or the marriages. The only reason I know the names of the women is that they are listed in later revision lists as the names of the spouses. Note that a common alternate name for "Itsko" is "Issac" (or Yitzhak in Hebrew).

Fourth generation (Arie Leib PITUM):

Beniamin and Sora had three children, one son and two daughters. The oldest of the children was their daughter Beyla, born in 1840 when her parents were 27 and 26 years old. Their son, Arie Leib, was born in 1846, and their second daughter, Rocha was born in 1852, when her father was 39 years old.

As is true for the earlier generations, there is still no specific information about this generation of Pitums.

It is this generation and the 1858 Revision List that provided a key link in tracing the ancestry of the Pitum family. As discussed in the introduction to this conjectural genealogy, Arie Leib is listed on one of the revision lists under the name "Aron" rather than "Arie". I believe that they are the same individual given the preponderance of the evidence, the consistency of the dates and names, as well as the relatively few Pitum families that existed in Stakliskes.

75

Fifth generation (Berka PITUM):

There is no further information about Beyla and Rocha, the two daughters of Beniamin and Sora.

Arie Lieb married a woman named Feiga. Their marriage produced at least one son: Berka Pitum, born in 1891 when his father was a relatively old 45 (alternative information indicates a birth year of 1889 when his father would have been 43). Given the scarcity of information, there may have been other children; Feiga could conceivably be a second wife. Berka Pitum also was known by the names Berka, Beryl and Dov Ber.

Berka Pitum is my father's father, or my grandfather.

Sixth generation (Feivel PITUM):

Berka Pitum married Asnat Baron. She was born in 1890, and is listed as being born in the town of Traby, although her parents and other relatives all seem to have been born in Aukstadvaris. Perhaps she was born during a brief visit away from Aukstadvaris. Clearly she was living in Aukstadvaris when she married Berka Pitum.

Although Berka Pitum was born in Stakliskes, he relocated to the nearby town of Aukstadvaris no later than the time of his marriage to Asnat. The wedding took place on March 13, 1914, when she was 24 and he was either 23 or 25 depending upon which birth date information is correct.

The marriage ceremony was performed by Rabbi Ruvin (Reuven) Braz (Baraz). It was witnessed by two men: Nesanel Keidanski and Iudel Zon (with "Zon" usually meaning "son of", in this case "son of Iudel"). Payment to the rabbi was 75 rubles. Berka's first cousin once removed was Iudel Wulf, although he was about 40 years older than Berka. If Iudel's son was also named Iudel (which would be possible if Iudel died sometime during the pregnancy of his wife), then this could be the person who was the witness at the marriage ceremony.

76

With respect to my grandmother, Asnat Baron, her parents were named Rachel Miller and Rael (Rachmil) Baron. One of Asnat's brothers was Julius Baron, who ultimately immigrated to the United States ahead of Feivel Pitum and sponsored his trip to the US and his immigration to his new country.

The children of the marriage of Berka and Asnat were Feivel, Leah and Rachel Feiga. Rachel Feiga was murdered near the end of 1940, ahead of her parents.

Leah managed to survive the killings and ultimately spent many years continuing to live in Lithuania under the Soviet Union's regime, finally immigrating to Israel, passing away in 1991 while living in Tel Aviv.

Both Berka and Asnat were murdered in Aukstadvaris in 1941, although a few months apart. The details are sketchy but my grandparents and my Aunt Rachel unfortunately became a part of the annihilation of Lithuanian Jewry.

Feivel Pitum went on to become my father, Philip Halpern. Leah Pitum went on to emigrate to Israel, become Leah Lazkovich, and become the mother of my two first cousins: Zalman and Asia Lazkovich.

Seventh Generation (Barry HALPERN):

Leah Pitum was married twice. Her first husband was Shtukarevich and he was killed during World War II. She remarried in 1946 a man named Lazkovich. Their marriage produced two children: Zalman, born in 1947 and Asia, born in 1952. Zalman and Asia are my first cousins.

Feivel Pitum, renamed Philip Halpern, married my mother, Minnie Waldman, on June 15, 1950. Their marriage produced one child, me – Barry Simon Halpern – born on November 23, 1952.

Eighth Generation (Philip, Peter and Lisa HALPERN):

Barry Halpern married Ellen Zaslaw on December 24, 1972. Our marriage produced three children. Philip, born

---

January 22, 1978; Peter, born October 5, 1979; Lisa, born February 9, 1982. My son Philip is named after his grandfather and holds the Hebrew/Yiddish name of Shraga Feivel (Ben Dov Ber).

Zalman Lazkovich married Ella Lenderman and their marriage produced two children: Anita, born 1978 and Lior, born 1982.

Asia Lazkovich married Misha Levit and their marriage produced two children: Anat, born 1982 and Guy, born 1985.

Zalman and Ella had been living in Toronto, Canada though are in the process of relocating back to Israel, where their children also live. Asia and her family all live in Israel.

The Halpern family all lives in Colorado, with Barry and Ellen living in Boulder, and Philip, Peter and Lisa living in their own homes in Westminster.

TIMELINE/KEY EVENTS

FOR FEIVEL PITUM/PHILIP HALPERN

March 13, 1914 – Feivel's parents, Berka Pitum and Asnat Baron, married in Aukstadvaris, Lithuania

July 19, 1915 – Feivel Pitum born in Aukstadvaris, Lithuania

1920s to 1933 – Feivel attends school in Lithuania, including the University of Lithuania in Kovno

1933, summer – Feivel attends a summer "camp", possibly a Gordonia (Zionist) camp in Stoklishok

April 29, 1934 – Feivel arrives in the port of Boston after sailing from Liverpool on the ship *"Britannic"*

1934 – Name became "Philip Halpern" though specific date unknown

1934 to 1941 – worked for Baron Dress Company

December 10, 1940 – sister Rachel murdered at age 17

March 19, 1941 – drafted into United States Army; met Isadore Zack

September 30, 1941 – father Berka murdered, probably in Trakai

1941 – mother Asnat murdered, probably in Trakai

December 18, 1942 – became naturalized US citizen in Miami, Florida

October 21, 1945 – honorable discharge from US Army

1945 to 1950 (?) – worked for Baron Dress Company

June 15, 1950 – married Minnie Jeannette Waldman in Wellesley, Massachusetts

November 23, 1952 – Barry Halpern born

1962 – moved from Dorchester (Boston) to Milton, Massachusetts

January 23, 1966 – died of a heart attack in Milton, Massachusetts

SAMPLE WRITINGS OF PHILIP HALPERN

The following pages contain samples of my father's writings. Some were published in newsletters, while others were taken from his letters and notes. I have deliberately done little or no editing of his writings as I wanted to present them as he wrote them.

As I've read and re-read his articles, I continue to be struck by how prescient he was. Many of his writings are as relevant today as they were in the 1960s. I admit that I'm biased, but I believe his skill in formulating and communicating his ideas and beliefs was truly extraordinary. He was certainly opinionated and never afraid to speak or write his mind. Sometimes he was harsh and at other times very gentle and sensitive. He was always passionate.

Source: Jeremiah Prophet - Jeremiah Lodge No 2063, B'Nai B'Rith

Volume VII Number VIII - April, 1963

ONE MAN'S OPINION by Phil Halpern

WHY ADULT JEWISH EDUCATION...Learning throughout life is basic in the traditions of Judaism.

One of the principal causes for the survival of the Jewish people throughout the ages is our Culture and Heritage.

In our time, however, study on the part of Adult Jews has been neglected or shall we say an "I don't care" attitude has evolved. Most Jews today are pathetically uninformed in the matter of Jewish culture...and, if possible, his children know less.

The adult Jew presents a strange paradox to the world...a man who knows all literature except his own...all philosophies but that of his own people.

We read books in twenty-nine tongues but we generally cannot understand a word of Hebrew.

We have plenty of time, it seems, to watch "The Defenders" on TV but have no time to learn about the "Defenders" of our own heritage.

We build structures of steel and stone but fail to build the minds of Jewish men. We devote our efforts to the education of our children, but fail to realize that the child honors only the ideals and practices of his parents.

Deeper concepts must be understood by mature men before they can be transmitted to the oncoming generations. The failure is all the more serious in the light of the challenges now confronting Judaism and the Jewish way of life.

In the determining of our future, the development of knowledgeable Jews is vital and could well prove decisive.

The world will be the loser if the Jewish traditions and culture vanishes, for in that event, there will have been eliminated from the human spirit a unique and irreplaceable color which has lent so much and has so much more to lend to the beauty of the world.

For this reason the program of Adult Jewish Education by B'nai B'rith is very important; it is dedicated to our religious heritage and the study of Jewish life.

I hope that in the future members of Jeremiah Lodge will take a more active part in the development of Adult Jewish Education so that we can get a better participation at our Adult Jewish Education meetings, rather than the lucky "seven" who attended the last March meeting.

There is no "Negro Problem" - from handwritten notes

Ashley Montague, famous anthropologist, said "When the white man talks about the Negro Problem", he really means the "white problem".

Negroes do not create problems in interpersonal relations, but the white man does.

What the Negro wants could never, under decent times create problems in human relations.

The Negro wants the right to live and to realize the best that is within him.

I ask in all fairness, is that a claim which is unreasonable?

What the Negro wants is to have the opportunity shared by all other men, to be treated as a human being who is neither better nor worse than other men. Is such a wish asking too much?

Should the right to vote, the right to a fair trial, the right to live as a citizen of the USA with all the rights granted to all other citizens, is that a "Negro problem?"

Why is it, then, that one particular group in these United States is forcibly deprived from these elementary rights?

It is the white man who creates those problems, not the black man.

In Europe, the pattern was the same except that in Europe, the absence of Negroes made it necessary to deal with minority groups that were available. I am sure everyone knows who was available - of course the Jews. I saw without any reservation, if there had been no Negroes in the United States, the Wallaces, Barnets, Bull Connors, and Faul-ass, would have used the Jews as scapegoats instead.

In Germany, there was no "Jewish problem". There was a "Hitler problem".

In the USA, there is no "Negro problem", there is a white citizen, Ku Klux, Eastland, Wallace, Perez problem"

83

It is the OPPRESSOR, not the victim who creates problems.

Jim Crowe laws and so-called "Southern customs" must be abolished.

Finally, the Negro should realize that he is not alone. He has many friends among US whites, who are with him all the way - to their complete FREEDOM...!

As a B'nai B'rith member, as an ADL chairman, I say if there is no freedom for the Negro there is no freedom for all of us.

1964 - from handwritten draft in notebook - "As I See It"

An inmate of an insane asylum is convinced that everybody else is crazy, except himself. Let us look at the facts...

In the 20th century, we in the Western world have created a greater material wealth than any other society in the history of the human race. Yet millions of people have been killed in an arrangement which we call "war". After the slaughter is over the enemies have become friends and the friends become enemies.

In the year 1964, we are prepared for a mass slaughter which would surpass any slaughter the human race has known.

In the year 1964, we are not behaving differently from what the civilized past of mankind has done in the last three thousand years of history.

In the year 1964 our economic affairs are scarcely more encouraging. We live in an economic system where we often restrict some of our agricultural productivity, although there are millions of people who do not have the very things we restrict, and who need them badly, because they are hungry.

In the year 1964, we have radio, television, movies, newspapers, but instead of giving us the best of past and present, these media of communication supplemented by advertising fill the minds of men with the cheapest trash, lacking in any sense of reality, and any suggestion of the production of movies and radio or television programs which would enlighten and improve the minds of our people would be met with indignation and accusations in the name of freedom and idealism.

What is the answer? I don't have the answer but I do know that man can protect himself from his own madness only by creating rather than by destroying.

A small tribe was told centuries ago: "I put before you life and death, blessing and curse - and you chose life."

Isn't this our choice?

It's Amazing - from handwritten notes

Let's face it, it's among Christians whom Jews reside. They are rarely aware of the Jew unless he hurts them. The Jew is silent and constant work for their welfare - one would almost think it doesn't exist.

Were it not for Jewish discoverers in medicine, millions of their children and people might have perished.

For two thousand years, the Western world has stopped the Jew from owning land, and then they have accused him of refusing to work it. They stopped him from bearing arms, and they called him a coward; they kept him from their schools and laughed at his ignorance. They kept him from public office and the right to vote and then they called him subversive and disloyal....isn't it amazing?

And still their every church is a monument to the Jew, Joshua ben Joseph and his apostles - Saul -whom they named Paul; Shimon who they named Peter; Levi, whom they named Matthew, and so on...

The Hebrew testament was the light and guide of Christianity.

Our greatest statesmen and reformers, men like Thomas Jefferson, Abraham Lincoln, held the Hebrew Testament to be the truth forever.

It's amazing!

Passover Thoughts

Through the ages, Passover has meant many things to the Jews. To some it means the Festival of Spring. To some the winter is gone. To some it meant adaptation to new conditions after they were exiled from Palestine. When the Temple was destroyed, it meant the transfer of observances to the home.

Known to us as "the Seder", is this our way that Jewish at home life was strengthened and in some way it compensated for the world's mistreatment to us.

Even the skeptic, cynic, the Jewish agnostic returned for this observance. Passover is also known as "Zman Cherusenu" - the season of our freedom.

Every Jew felt he was liberated. This great emancipation has not taken hold only of Jewish history but mankind. It played a role in the American Revolution.

On the very day when independence was declared, a seal was selected for the new nation by Franklin, Adams and Jefferson, the design represented the Egyptians drawing in the Red Sea, as Moses was leading the Jews to freedom and the inscription read "rebellion against tyrants is obedience to God".

On the American Liberty Bell is a saying not of the American but of Moses "Proclaim liberty throughout the land and to all the inhabitants thereof".

So you see there is more than Matzot, Kneidlach to Pesach.

The following is a tribute to our late president, John F Kennedy, written in the form of a letter by a son to his father, by Phil Halpern

Friday, November 22, 1963

Dear Dad

President Kennedy's death made me think of Passover, when we sit at the Seder and I ask you the Four Questions. Only on this tragic night, I have more than four questions to ask.

President Kennedy searched for peace....
Why did they assassinate the peacemaker?
President Kennedy was a vigorous leader....
Why then did the bullet strike him?
President Kennedy loved his children and family...
Why then did they kill the father?
President Kennedy advised the young smart people to enter politics...

Why then did they destroy the smartest of them all?

President Kennedy was always on the lookout for American security...

Why then did they kill the commander in chief?

President Kennedy fought for good education for all....
Why then was he taken away from us?
President Kennedy fought for equal rights for all Americans...

Why then did they kill the greatest American of them all?

Please Dad, answer my questions. I am so confused!!

Love,

Your son...

The father's reply:

Dear Son,
I have been searching for answers to your questions, but to no avail.

Please forgive me, son, as I am confused too.

Love,

Your father

Why Is It?

Date unknown; original title appears to have been "The

Bible and the Twist"

Why is it that man permits indignities to be done to man?

Why is it that there is a group of countries including Yemen, Saudi Arabia and Alecimia(?) that either deals in slaves, or keeps them. For "oily" reasons the Western world has done little to wipe out this barbaric practice but instead it deals with bearded crooked heads.

Why is it that man allows it to happen? Have you ever heard the white preachers from down south quoting the bible to support grandpappy's enslavement of the black man?

Of course grandpappy is dead now, but there are his grandchildren who at this writing, walk into eating places where no black man will be served. They congregate in church, but no nigger may pass through. There is a little door in the back marked "for colored only". I wonder if Peter the Gate keeper has such a back door.

Why is it that man can stomach this and find nothing wrong in it?

Why don't you know" said the preacher to the rabbi. It says in the gospels "give to Caesar what is Caesar's". The rabbi astounded asked "but how about the love for thy neighbors". And the preacher replied "we sure love them poor creatures, but we love them, black, ugly, dumb and loyal the way God made them.

Why is it flattering to man's soul to be considered better than a whole race of people, be it Jewish race or the African race or the Chinese is something I'll never understand. Why is it….?

90

A Controversial Play

Der Stellvertreter (Deputy)

On February 27, 1964 on West 47th Street in New York City a group of pickets marched in front of a theater. Among the pickets were Catholics, Protestants, Jews. The pickets included, believe it or not, 15 members of the American Nazi Party. They were protesting the showing of Hochutti's controversial drama "the deputy". "The Deputy" attacks Pope Pius XII for having failed to take a strong stand in condemning the Nazi murder of the Jews in World War II.

The signs carried by the Nazi trooper read "the play is anti-Catholic" and "Jews mock Pius XII".

A Jew did not write the play. A Protestant German did, author Rolf Hochuth.

The play had its premier in West Berlin and became the most controversial, sought after play in Europe. In Paris the performance was interrupted. In Switzerland the actors were hooted or cheered. It has been playing in every major city in Europe.

The play has produced libel suits, threats and picketing by what must surely be one of the strangest groups of bedfellows in history - Jewish and Catholic Veterans group and George Lincoln Rockwell. The battle is over the interpretation of the fact, over the Pope's motives for remaining silent.

The defenders of the Pope assert that he refrained because a public declaration would have provoked more Nazi persecution. The play, however, brings out the fact that the Pope, the only neutral leader of Christendom should have raised against the most frightful immorality in all history - Genocide. None of the major secular Jewish groups - the American Jewish Congress, the American Jewish Committee and the Anti-Defamation Leagues - has taken a formal public position on the play, as all have experienced internal divisions over it.

—

Israeli reaction to the play has been tempered by extreme caution. They want it performed but they think it is not the time.

One thing is sure: the play has ruffled the dignity of the Vatican and troubled the conscience of the Christians.

To me it seems the play is against Germany and against the Pope. Germany for allowing it to raise a Hitler.

It condemns the Pope for not helping enough because the Pope did help the Jews, but on the other hand he did not do any more than ordinary decent men in the street, and because he was the leader of 500 million Catholics we expected more from him...

Jeremiah Prophet
Volume VII Number III

November, 1963

ADL (Anti-Defamation League) Report by Philip Halpern
"A Jew Looks Toward the Ecumenical Council"
Attention should be given to the courageous efforts being made by Catholic leaders in facing the problems of the modern world.

Popes John and Paul have, with the support of the progressive church elements in most countries of the world, so far managed to achieve a series of enactments in the liberal spirit.

One of the pressing subjects with which the new secretariat, headed by the progressive Jesuit Cardinal Bea, will have to deal, is the relationship between Catholics and Jews.

Many Jewish organizations have urged the Vatican to seize this opportunity for a binding pronouncement.

It must be remembered however, that the Council's terms of reference are essentially religious and contributions that could be made would probably lie in the field of DOGMA.

It is precisely in the field of DOGMA that the Council can play an important role.

What is called for is more than a mere denunciation of anti-semitism...a clear reinterpretation of one of the darkest chapters of the Catholic doctrine; the condemnation of the Jews to eternal punishment for their rejection of Christ...apart from the obvious fact that Jesus' early supporters were, like himself, Jewish.

The church should have the courage to insist that the teaching of this period be reformed so as to ensure a proper historical perspective on the one hand, and to fight the traditional doctrine whereby contemporary Jews are identified with the Jews depicted in the final scenes of the Gospels.

The anti-Jewish myth created by these teachings has been the most malignant root of Western anti-semitism.

93

It is more relevant to question their relationship to the destruction of Europe's Jews, than the part played by the silence of Pope Pius XII during the Nazi era.

By facing this problem with the same courage as he has already displayed in other directions, Pope Paul will earn the gratitude, not only of Jews, but of humanity as well.

Editorial by Phil Halpern – Jeremiah Lodge Newsletter
(date unknown)

"I CHARGE THE WHITE MAN WITH BEING THE GREATEST LIAR ON EARTH!!

I CHARGE THE WHITE MAN WITH BEING THE GREATEST DECEIVER ON EARTH!!

An   all   Negro   jury...Verdict....GUILTY!! Sentence.....DEATH!!

This is the finale of a play produced and directed by members of a growing sect named "The Temple of Islam". They are more commonly called "Black Muslims".

They are anti-white and anti-semitic. They are also dedicated and disciplined.

"The Muslims" are a "NATIONAL THREAT", said the Mayor of Los Angeles to Attorney General Robert F. Kennedy.

The Los Angeles Chief of Police said that the situation is "REAL DYNAMITE".

This situation exists in many other cities across the country. Responsible and established Negroes have spoken out against the "Muslims".

Unquestionably, the momentum of the Temple of Islam movement has increased in recent years within the Negro communities. This rise in prestige is noted in the "Muslim" condemnation of the white man and glorification of the "Black Race".

What is the Temple of Islam?"

The "Muslims" beliefs are a blend of racism and Islam, with Wallace D. Ford as the "Incarnation of Allah"....."and Allah will rescue the black people from the oppression.

"America is the place where Allah will make himself felt". This is the cry of Elijah Muhammad, who calls himself the spiritual leader of the Lost-Found nation in the west. His headquarters are in Chicago. According to Mohammed, all negroes are divine, all white men are devils.

The question of how "Moslem" the "Muslims" are not clear at all. As a matter of fact Muslim Racism clearly flaunts the basic Moslem doctrine that all men, regardless of color, are brothers. The Muslims preach that the white man oppresses the black man. The white man must be wiped out because he is "false".

Rep. Adam Clayton Powell, Harlem's voice in Congress, had some kind words to say about the "Muslims". "The Muslims are energetic and dedicated. They preach their doctrine anywhere."

The Muslims feed on widespread discontent among a people who seek some kind of change for the better.

IF THE MUSLIM IDEOLOGY CONTINUES TO SPREAD VIOLENCE COULD BE THE RESULT!

We, as B'nai B'rithers, would like ADL's view on this subject.

Miscellaneous Notes by Philip Halpern

There were apparently at least two showing of movies that Isadore Zack asked Phil to attend and "report" on....

October 16, 1959 - letter asking several ADL chairman to attend the movie "The Rosary" and report back on its content and audience reaction.

October 24, 1959 - Philip attended the movie (with Minnie) at the new Catholic theater on Massachusetts Avenue (formerly "Loew's Theater". 100 people attended, mostly women and few children. Not much audience reaction at all. Phil's view of the movie was that it did not reflect prejudice and that he would respect the filmmakers for their beliefs.

There was a second movie called "The Sermon on the Mount". Phil said that it was "a hate film", intended to arouse hatred against Jews. "…As I left the theater on Saturday night, with my wife, that if I had not been there to see it, and to be a part of it, it would be difficult to believe that in the year 1959, in the land of the free, in the city of liberty where a Cardinal professes to be a friend of the Jews, where brotherhood dinners are televised, where at a testimonial dinner for a leading Rabbi the principle speaker will be the Cardinal, that a person can walk up to a theater, and for a dollar purchase a ticket and witness such a hate film. It made me sick to my stomach."

October 28, 1959- letter from Isadore Zack to Philip, thanking him for attending and reporting on the movie.

March 24, 1960 - letter from Isadore Zack asking Philip to see the movie again, though it is a different portion of the movie from the original. The concern is with the part relating to the crucifixion. His follow-up handwritten notes refer again to the hatred depicted and his concern that this is what is being taught to the children in Sunday school.

Date Unknown - from handwritten pages; appears to be taken from a journalist Alex Coler

What happened to Jews in the ghetto of Warsaw may have been worse, but I doubt it. The Universal Jewish Encyclopedia calls it "one of the most brutal pogroms in history."

I do remember the sick feeling I had in the pit of my stomach when I saw five fire engines arrive in front of a synagogue which had been set afire and the Legion of the Archangel Michael with guns forced the firemen to drive away.

Alex Coler

During the night members of the Legion, after praying and drinking some of each other's blood, went to the homes of some at Bucharest's most distinguished Jews and loaded nearly two hundred men and women into trucks. The victims were taken to the abattoir on the edge of the city. They were stripped naked, forced to get down on all fours, and were driven up the ramp of the slaughterhouse. Then they were put thru all the stages of animals at slaughter until finally the beheaded bodies, spurting blood, were hung on iron hooks along the wall. As a last sadistic touch the legionnaires took rubber stamps and branded the carcasses with the Rumanian equivalent of "fit for human consumption".

I made a silent promise that as long as I lived I would devote at least part of my time and energy toward trying to atone, to the Jews of the world who survived, for the sins committed on the edge of Bucharest, Rumania by men who knew better for them had been at least exposed to the Christian precepts of humility, gentility and non-violence.

The worst part of it was that they had done it with prayers on their lips, and crosses and crucifixes on their hands or hanging on their necks.

Selection of Written exchanges between Isadore Zack and Philip Halpern

November 16, 1959 - letter from Isadore Zack to Phil, asking for help in promoting a new fair housing law. In addition to support in promoting the law, Phil's chapter of B'nai B'rith is being asked for a $15 contribution towards an overall $800 budget.

December 9, 1959 - letter from Isadore Zack thanking Phil for a $5 contribution.

December 21, 1959 - letter from Isadore Zack to Phil regarding an incorrect newspaper story which stated that Hull B'nai B'rith was holding a "Christmas Party" for "retarded children on the south shore". Apparently Phil had raised the issue, and had been involved in clarifying it.

January 5, 1960 - letter from Isadore Zack referring to an incident at the Girls Latin School that must have had something to do with anti-Semitism. Apparently Philip's involvement in raising the issue led to meetings with school administration and commitments to future work groups to promote understanding.

January 18, 1960 - general letter referring to upcoming meetings regarding anti-semitic incidents and how to deal with them.

February 9, 1960 - letter from Isadore Zack to Philip regarding a recent meeting that Phil held, and Isadore spoke at, regarding anti-semitic incidents (relating to the use of swastikas).

Undated from ADL - regarding proposed new laws dealing with defacing of educational or religious properties

November 7, 1961 - letter from Isadore Zack requesting that Philip attend a meeting at John Hancock Hall in Boston, of a "reactionary group". The group is called the "American Institute Inc" - with commentator Fulton Lewis, Jr.

May 7, 1965 - letter from ADL regarding "revision and liberalization" of US immigration laws.

Letter from Isadore Zack (ADL) dated December 9, 1959 - he thanks Phil for a $5 contribution. Seems that he donated despite not having enough money.

Letter from Iz Zack on December 21, 1959 to Phil - Seems that Phil had complained about a newspaper story that the Hull chapter of B'nai B'rith was going to hold a party for "retarded children" and that the paper said it was a "Christmas Party". Iz apparently checked into this and said that everyone involved was embarrassed at the miscommunication. It was a secular party having nothing to do with Christmas.

Several different letters are referring to the ADL and involvement in anti-semitic incidents in the Boston area. This includes the Girls' Latin School. In one letter, Iz asks Phil to see a movie on March 29, 1960 at the Loew's State on Mass Ave - the movie is "The Rosary" and the ADL had several complaints about it. (I can't find anything about it in the IMDB)

December, 1965 - event to celebrate Hanukah (my cousins Joyce and Barry Shane)

Today, the world over, Jews celebrate Hanukah. In Jewish homes the story of triumph of the Maccabees is told once again, and the Hanukah candles glow again.

Hanukah is the story of triumph of right over might.

Without diminishing the festival spirits in the slightest, this commemoration is of special significance to every Jew, but more meaningful to us in B'nai B'rith...for are we not in a sense Maccabees? Twentieth Century Maccabees if you please...but Maccabees nonetheless.

They were fighting for freedom of worship. They were fighting to liberate the spirit of enslaved people. They were fighting for human freedom and dignity...A struggle which we continue to pursue for all of humanity through B'nai B'rith.

As we light our Hanukah candles tonight let us rededicate to the ideals of our faith, let us bring the light of our menorah into the lives of others.

In keeping with the spirit of Hanukah, may I introduce the first part of our program, which is a musical one.

A trio of two young men and a young lady, who will sing for us Hebrew and Israeli songs.

Paul Shane studied in the Hebrew University and is now a student at BU majoring in sociology.

Barry Shane, his brother, is graduate assistant to the Dean of Research Administration at Northeastern,

And his lovely wife, Joyce, who studied at Hebrew University, graduated from Barnard College in New York and is a geologist.

In addition they are all students at Hebrew Teachers College.

Ladies and Gentlemen, the Shane Trio!

Biography of Isadore Zack – circa August, 1961

Isadore Zack is Civil Rights Director of the New England Regional Office of the Anti-Defamation League of B'nai B'rith. In this capacity, Mr Zack is in charge of the fact-finding activities of the League in this area. The ADL, educational arm of B'nai B'rith, oldest and largest Jewish service organization in the world, is engaged in a program designed to strengthen the democratic fabric of the American community by working with church, school, civic, and other local and national groups in a joint effort to eradicate racial and religious discrimination. Its fact finding department investigates and reports on the activities of the professional hate mongers and bigots, seeking to check their undemocratic practices by exposing them to the light of public opinion.

Mr Zack came to the ADL in 1946, directly after five years service with the US Army in WWII, four of those years being spent with the Military Intelligence Division as a Special Agent. For three years he was Special Agent in charge of the Counter Intelligence Group for the First Service Command, and as such was commended by the Secretary of War for outstanding service, one of six citations he received. He is currently Secretary of the Military Intelligence Association of New England. Mr Zack is vice president of the National Counter Intelligence Corps Association.

ADL (Anti-Defamation League) speakers introduced by Philip at breakfast meetings

Ephraim Isaac

March 31, 1965 - a breakfast meeting with Ephraim Isaac as the speaker. From his letter of introduction: "I studied philosophy and music as an undergraduate, and am presently a graduate student at the Graduate School of Arts and Sciences at Harvard. I also am Chairman of the Ethiopian Literacy Campaign."

His speaking topic was the Hebraic-Jewish influences on Ethiopian culture. "For instance, Ethiopians circumcise their children; they abstain from unclean food; they keep the Sabbath; Ethiopian churches are built in the manner of Solomon's temple.

From Philip's written notes of introduction:

"The Ethiopian chronicle relates that the Queen of Sheba during her visit to King Solomon in Jerusalem, conceived a son whose father was Solomon, that the son was named Memilek and that he became the founder of the Royal Dynasty of Ethiopia.

Ethiopia's 3000 year history has been dominated by the principle of freedom and the ancient civilization is proud of its tradition.

I am sure you all remember the glorious fight by the Lion of Judah Hailie Selassie, against the Italians in the Second World War.

Our speaker is a native from Ethiopia. He has written a paper on his country and on Judaism. He studied philosophy and music as an undergraduate and presently is a graduate student at the Graduate School of Arts and Sciences at Harvard.

It is an honor and a privilege at this time that I present to you Mr Ephraim Isaac."

Following is the current biography of Ephraim Isaac, taken from the Encyclopedia of Ethiopia web page: http://www.ethiopedia.com/index.php?title=Ephraim_Isaac

Ephraim Isaac, BD (Harvard Divinity School '63), Ph.D. (Harvard University '69), D.H.L. (CUNY) D.Litt. (AAU), a founder and the first professor of Afro-American Studies at Harvard University when the Department was created in 1969, is author of numerous scholarly works about the Late Second Temple period and Classical Yemenite Jewish and Ethiopic religious literature. He is currently Director of the Institute of Semitic Studies, Princeton, NJ, Chair of the Board of the Horn of Africa Peace & Development Committee, and President of the Yemenite Jewish Federation of America. He has taught at Princeton University, Hebrew University, University of Pennsylvania, Bard College, and other institutions of higher learning. He has received many honors including the Tanenbaum Center for Interreligious Understanding's 2002 Peacemaker in Action Award, honorary degrees from John J. College of CUNY, Addis Ababa University of Ethiopia, NEH Fellowship, among others. He knows seventeen languages, and lectures widely on the subject of "Religion & Warfare", "Religion and Hate", etc. and sits on Boards of some twenty-five international religious, educational, and cultural organizations.

Currently, Professor Ephraim Isaac is the Director of the Institute of Semitic Studies in Princeton, NJ and Fellow of The Dead Sea Scrolls Foundation. Born in Ethiopia where he got his early education, Dr. Isaac holds a B. A. degree in Philosophy, Chemistry, & Music (Concordia College); a Master degree in Divinity (Harvard Divinity School); a Ph.D. in Near Eastern Languages (Harvard University. He was Professor at Harvard University between 1968 and 1977, the first professor hired in Afro-American Studies at Harvard, and one of its founders, he was voted the best teacher each year by the students and the Department.

In addition to his Harvard appointment that endowed the "Ephraim Isaac Prize" in African Studies in 1998, Dr. Isaac has lectured at Hebrew University, Princeton University, University of Pennsylvania, Howard University, Divinity School, Lehigh University, Bard College and other institutions of higher learning.

His areas of studies range from Biblical Hebrew, Rabbinic Literature, Ethiopian Religions and History, to Concept and History of Slavery and Ancient African Civilizations. He has been a Fellow of the National Endowment for the Humanities and the Institute for Advanced Studies. He has received many awards and honors including an Honorary D. H. L. (John Jay College, CUNY); the 2002 Peacemaker in Action Award of the Tanenbaum Center for Inter-religious Understanding; United Nation Association of Ethiopia Certificate of Appreciation, 2000; Education and Peace Merit Award of the Society of Ethiopians Established in Diaspora; and Ethiopian "Interfaith Peace-Building Initiative Decree of Merit, 2004; and many others.

Dr. Isaac is the author of numerous articles and books on (Late Second Temple) Jewish and (Ancient Ethiopic) Ge'ez literatures. Three of his works pertain to the oldest known manuscripts of The Book of Enoch (Doubleday, 1983) and An Ethiopic History of Joseph (Sheffield Press, 1990), and Proceedings of Second International Congress of Yemenite Jewish Studies (ISS & University of Haifa, 1999). An expanded definitive version of his The Ethiopian Orthodox Church is forthcoming. He is currently working on a new edition of the "Dead Sea Scrolls Fragments of The Book of Enoch" (Princeton Theological Seminary); "A History of Religions in Africa"; and "A Cultural History of Ethiopian Jews". He publishes and is on editorial board of the international scholarly journal on Afroasiatic Languages, Journal of Afroasiatic Languages (Cushitic, Semitic, Ancient Egyptian...), and sits on the Board of the Journal for the Study of thePseudepigrapha.

Dr. Isaac speaks seventeen languages. He is the first translator of Handel's Messiah into Amharic, Ethiopian official language and is widely known in Ethiopia as the founder of the National Literacy Campaign that made millions literate in the late sixties. Currently he is also the international Chair of the Horn of Africa Board of Peace and Development Organization (Addis Ababa, Asmara) and the President of The Yemenite Jewish Federation of America.

His father was a Yemenite Jew prominent in the Dire Dawa Jewish community and whose mother was an Ethiopian Christian who convened to Judaism. In 1937 he came to the United States for education, already knowing Oromigna, Amharic, Ge'ez, Hebrew, and English. In 1959 he became president of the Ethiopian Student Association in North America. He earned a Bachelor of Divinity degree from Harvard after graduating from Concordia College in Minnesota, then he received a Ph.D. from Harvard's Department of Near Eastern Languages and Civilizations. He has taught at Harvard, Princeton, the University of Pennsylvania, Hunter, Bard, Lehigh, and Hebrew University in Jerusalem. He is presently director of the Institute of Semitic Studies at Princeton and publishes the Journal of Afroasiatic Languages. He helped found the National Literacy Campaign in Ethiopia in the 1960s. As coordinator of the Ad Hoc Ethiopian Peace Committee, he participated in the July 1991 conference in Addis Ababa.

David Chajmowicz

The breakfast speaker for December 20, 1964 was David Chajmowicz, who spoke on "the status of the Jewish community in Cuba before, during and after Castro". According to a letter from Mr Chajmowicz, he lived in Cuba for 40 years, with five of these being under Castro. He was the organizer for B'nai B'rith in Havana and the first president of the Maimonides Lodge. He organized the Hillel Foundation at the Havana University. He was President of Ort in Havana, and was a member of the board of education of the Jewish school in Havana.

A subsequent internet search reveals that B'nai B'rith observed its 65th anniversary in Cuba in 2008, meaning that Mr Chajmowicz started the organization in 1943 during World War II. There are apparently between 600-1000 Jews living in Cuba currently, from a high of 15,000 just prior to Castro's taking over.

Pho Ba Hai

In a letter postmarked October 12, 1965, Phil received a resume from Pho Ba Hai, who was attending Boston University (age 29). The cover letter indicated that he would be speaking at the upcoming Sunday meeting (presumably October 17, 1965).

Pho Ba Hai listed Saigon as his address. He was completing a PhD apparently in public administration.

A Google search for Pho Ba Hai (Dr Hai Ba Pho) reveals that he went on to obtain his PhD with a doctoral dissertation on "the dominant characteristics of the South Vietnamese civil bureaucracy and the prismatic "Sala" model. This appears to have been published in 1972.

A photo of him appears from a funeral at which he spoke, in February 2009.

He was the author of at least three books regarding Vietnamese Public Management (published in 1999-2000), as well as papers and books on law.

He also is a Professor Emeritus at the University of Massachusetts in Lowell, and his degrees appear to have been earned from Boston College (rather than Boston University). He is/was (as of 2005) a member of the Vietnamese North American University Professor Network.

Haskell Kassler

On November 2, 1958 (Sunday) there was a Jeremiah Lodge meeting at Hadrath Israel Synagogue in Dorchester. Attorney Haskell Kassler spoke on his experience in Mississippi where he was beaten, arrested and jailed while representing civil rights workers.

Philip's brief handwritten note might have been a quote from Haskell Kassler:

"I do not consider this merely an honor to me personally, but a tribute to the discipline and wise restraint and majestic courage of the millions of gallant Negroes and whites of good will who have followed a nonviolent course in seeking to establish a reign of justice and a rule of love across this nation."

He is still alive (2010) and practicing in Boston. Apparently passed the bar in 1960 and currently is involved in family and probate law.

PEDIGREE CHART FOR FEIVEL PITUM – based on conjectural genealogical history

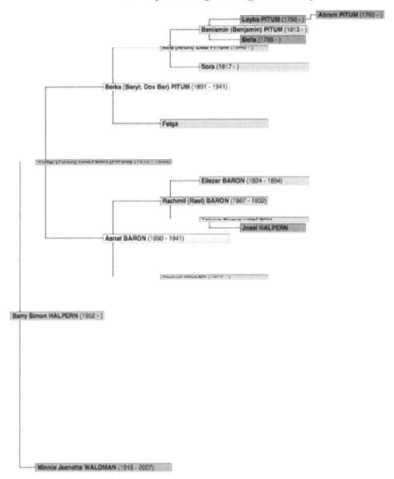

MISCELLANEOUS BACKGROUND AND FAMILY HISTORY INFORMATION FOR FEIVEL PITUM/PHILIP HALPERN FOR ABRAM PITUM

Military service facts:

1. army serial number 31031362, grade pfc
2. date of entry into service March 19, 1941
3. served as radio operator (low speed), interpreter, heavy mortar crewman (this is why he knew morse code)
4. Company M 157th infantry regiment
5. Sharpshooter Rifle - Marksman Carbine - Combat
6. Battles and campaigns: Rhineland, Central Europe
7. Decorations and Citations: Good Conduct Medal, American Defense Service Medal, European African Middle Eastern Theater Campaign Ribbon
8. Service outside US: October 6, 1944 arrived October 20, 1944 in European Theater; departed Europe September 3, 1945

Translated letter that Phil wrote on board ship en route to USA in 1934 (see original page 115); translation by Shai Kowitt

Sunday, 22 April 1934, Atlantic Ocean

Hi, Esther!

I wanted to know already what is going on with you, but one can't always get what one wants, since I can't receive letters from you at sea or on the road.

On Wednesday when I was in Hamburg I wrote you a postcard. On that day I left Hamburg and traveled on a small ship to England. The trip took 1 ½ days. I will write you the truth—I was seasick and spent the entire trip lying in bed and didn't eat anything, since a small ship really rocks back and forth a lot in the water. But when I reached the coast of England, I felt healthy again. I travelled by car to Liverpool. I spent a day in Liverpool, and on Saturday afternoon I was sitting on the "*Britannic*". And at 3 PM we said goodbye to Europe.

On a ship there are amazing things. In general everything here is made using the latest techniques. On the ship there is theater, movies, and anything you can imagine you will find on the ship. Only one thing is not here, and that is Esther...

I've passed through several countries and indeed there are things to see in the world. I want to write you more but I can't, but it is not my fault, my head hurts from travelling. When I get to America I'll write you more about everything, that is to say, about the entire journey.

Stay well, write me letters. When I get to America I hope I already find letters from you.

I truly wanted to write more, but I can't, because my head hurts me.

The translation of the draft letter continues...

To the "Gordonija" chapter in Baltimore: Attention!

This letter will certainly amaze you, since even though I don't know you, I nevertheless take the liberty of writing you a letter, since, first of all, I want to announce to you that I am a member of the "Gordonija" movement in Lithuania, just arrived this week in America, who organized the chapter in Lithuania, and now, having come to America, I'd like very much to familiarize myself with the movement and the active members here, since we in Lithuania are unfamiliar with the movement in America because of a lack of news. Write me a letter right away and if you, dear friends/comrades, wish, I can ...<illegible>

Even though I don't know you, I nevertheless have the responsibility [he might mean "authority"] to write you a letter.

First of all, I want to let you know that I am a member of the "Gordonija" movement in Lithuania, who has arrived just this week in America. I am one of the members who worked and labored on a field in "Eretz Yisrael Ovedet" [Land of Israel Youth Labor Movement] in Lithuania in general and for our movement in particular.

Now that I've come to America, I'd like to become acquainted with you and establish permanent communications so that I can continue my work for our movement here in America.

Secondly, I wanted to get news about our movement in America that we members in Lithuania are unfamiliar with, simply for want of news.

As far as I know, a "Gordonija" branch in Boston exists, but I don't have the address.

Continuing with an alternate draft...

Dear friends/comrades, I am writing to you this letter first of all because of my responsibility to the movement and secondly because the last time I was at headquarters in Lithuania, the members of the board asked me to make contact with you and take an active role in our work in America.

113

I am quite familiar with the state of America Jews; and in general working under such conditions for Eretz Yisrael HaOvedet in general, and in particular for our movement as it prepares for collective life in Israel, requires courage.

Therefore, comrades, we must assess/appreciate the difficult situation in which the Jewish people in general and our movement in particular are found now and not miss the opportunity that the moment presents; and we must work with the maximum energy.

The success in establishing Gordonija chapters, sustaining our work in America, is our success.

In the same vein, I've brought material so that we can conduct necessary work.

I end my short letter with the hope that you will be able to fulfil my request and reply a.s.a.p. I'll write you more in the next letter.

With the blessing of rain,
Your friend/comrade/fellow member,
Shraga Pitum
Please write letters to this address:

Mr. Julius Baron 21 James St.

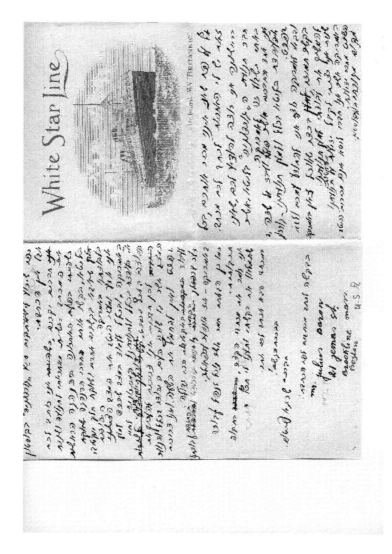

Draft letter written on the Britannic

Lithuania – from Vilna to Troki to Aukstadvaris to Stakliskes
Source: Google maps

Lithuania – A, B, C, D are cities mentioned in text
Source: Google maps

The Central Database of Shoah Victims' Names

Testimony Page from Yad Vashem – Ber Pitum

The Central Database of Shoah Victims' Names
Yad Vashem
Яд Вашем
About Us | The Holocaust | Digital Collections Education & E-learning | Exhibitions | Donate | Righteous | Visiting | YV Worldwide
Русский | עברית

Full Record Details for Pitumas Berelis

Source	Pages of Testimony
Last Name	PITUMAS
Last Name	PITUM
First Name	BERELIS
First Name	DOV
First Name	BERL
First Name*	BER
Father's First Name	ARIE
Father's First Name	LEB
Mother's First Name	FEIGA
Gender	Male
Place of Birth	AUKSTADVARIS, TRAKAI, LITHUANIA
Marital Status	MARRIED
Spouse's First Name*	ASNAT
Spouse's Maiden Name	BRUN
Permanent Place of Residence	AUKSTADVARIS, TRAKAI, LITHUANIA
Profession	FACTORY OWNER
Place of Death	TROKI WILNO, WILNO, POLAND
Date of Death	30/9/1941
Age	52
Type of material	Page of Testimony
Submitter's Last Name	SAFIRSHTEIN
Submitter's First Name	YAAKOV
Relationship to victim	COMMUNITY MEMBER
קרבת משפחה	PITUMAS, PITUM, RAKHEL, FEIGA

* Indicates an automatic Translation From Hebrew
The Names Database is a work in progress and may contain errors that shall be corrected in the near future.

Translation of Testimony Page for Ber Pitum

Testimony Page from Yad Vashem – Asnat Baron Pitum

The Central Database of Shoah Victims' Names

About Us | The Holocaust | Digital Collections | Education & E-learning | Exhibitions | Donate | Righteous | Visiting | YV World

Русский | עברית

Full Record Details for **Pitumieni Asnat**

Source	Pages of Testimony
Last Name	PITUMIENI
Last Name	PITUM
First Name*	ASNAT
Father's First Name	YERAKHMIEL
Mother's First Name	RAKHEL
Gender	Female
Place of Birth	ALKSTADVARIS, TRAKAI, LITHUANIA
Marital Status	MARRIED
Permanent Place of Residence	ALKSTADVARIS, TRAKAI, LITHUANIA
Profession	HOUSEWIFE
Place of Death	TROKI, WILNO WILNO, POLAND
Date of Death	1941
Age	53
Type of material	Page of Testimony
Submitter's Last Name	SAFIRSHTEIN
Submitter's First Name	YAAKOV
Relationship to victim	COMMUNITY MEMBER
(עברית)	PITUMIENI, PITUM, RAKHEL, FEIGA

* Indicates an automatic Translation From Hebrew

The Names Database is a work in progress and may contain errors that shall be corrected in the near future.

Translation of Testimony Page for Asnat Baron

Testimony Page from Yad Vashem – Rachel Pitum

The Central Database of Shoah Victims' Names

About Us | The Holocaust | Digital Collections | Education & E-learning | Exhibitions | Donate | Righteous | Visiting | YV Worldwide

Pycckий | עברית

Full Record Details for **Pitumaite Rachela**

Source		Pages of Testimony	
Last Name		PITUMAITE	
Last Name		PITUM	
First Name		RACHELA	
First Name		RAKHEL	
Father's First Name		DOV	
Mother's First Name		AGNAT	
Gender		Female	
Date of Birth		1923	
Place of Birth		AUKSTADVARIS, TRAKAI, LITHUANIA	
Marital Status		SINGLE	
Permanent Place of Residence		AUKSTADVARIS, TRAKAI, LITHUANIA	
Profession		SALESWOMAN IN A STORE	
Place during the war		LITHUANIA	
Place of Death		TROKI, WILNO, WILNO, POLAND	
Date of Death		12/18/1940	
Type of material		Page of Testimony	
Submitter's Last Name		KATZ	
Submitter's First Name		ZELIG	
Relationship to victim		FRIEND	

' Indicates an automatic Translation From Hebrew

The Names Database is a work in progress and may contain errors that shall be corrected in the near future.

Translation of Testimony Page for Rachel Pitum

1934 Britannic Manifest for Feivel Pitum

BIBLIOGRAPHY AND SOURCES

1. Beider, Alexander. *A Dictionary of Jewish Surnames from the Russian Empire.* Avotaynu, 1993.
2. Boxerman, Benita and Burton. *Jews and Baseball: Volume I: Entering the American Mainstream, 1871-1948.* Mcfarland and Company. 2006.
3. Greenbaum, Masha. *The Jews of Lithuania: A History of a Remarkable Community 1316-1945.* Gefen Publishing House, Ltd, 1995.
4. Katz, Dovid. *Lithuanian Jewish Culture.* Central European University Press, 2010.
5. Levin, Dov. *The Litvaks: A Short History of the Jews in Lithuania.* Yad Vashem Pubns, 2001.
6. Oshry, Ephraim. *Annihilation of Lithuanian Jewry.* Judaica Press, 1995.
7. Spector, Shmuel, and Geoffrey Wigoder. *The Encyclopedia of Jewish Life Before and During the Holocaust.* Ed. Shmuel Spector, and Geoffrey Wigoder. New York University Press, 2001.
8. Sutton, Karen. *The Massacre of the Jews of Lithuania.* Geffen Publishing House, 2008.
9. Various web sites containing US census data, ship manifests, death records, etc. - Ancestry.com, Jewishgen.org, footnote.com, ellieisland.org, stevemorse.org
10. *Encyclopedia of Ethiopia web page: http://www.ethiopedia.com/index.php?title=Ephraim_Is aac*
11. The LitvakSIG (special interest group) under Jewishgen
12. The US Holocaust Memorial Museum web site (source of the Gordonia photo from 1933)
13. Yadvashem.org - source of the pages of testimony
14. Wikipedia
15. Translators: Shai Kowitt; Jack Welner

Made in the USA
Charleston, SC
01 August 2011